READINGS ON EQUAL EDUCATION
(Formerly *Educating the Disadvantaged*)

ADVISORY PANEL

READINGS ON EQUAL EDUCATION

Volume 14

FORTY YEARS AFTER THE *BROWN* DECISION: SOCIAL AND CULTURAL EFFECTS OF SCHOOL DESEGREGATION

Co-Editors
Charles Teddlie
Kofi Lomotey

Managing Editors
John Freeman
Robin Jarvis

AMS PRESS
NEW YORK

Copyright © 1997 by AMS Press, Inc.
All rights reserved.

Library of Congress Catalogue Number 77-83137
International Standard Book Number: Set 0-404-10100-3
International Standard Book Number: Vol.14: 0-404-10114-3
International Standard Series Number: 0270-1448

All AMS Books are printed on acid-free paper that meets the guidelines for performance and durability of the Committee on Production
Guidelines for Book Longevity of the Council On Library Resources.

Manufactured in the United States of America

AMS Press, Inc.
56 East 13th Street
New York, N.Y. 10003

VOLUME 14

VOLUME 13

Section II. The Impact of Desegregation on Black Colleges

ROBERT L. CRAIN is a professor of sociology and education at Columbia University's Teachers College and an expert on school desegregation and race relations. He is first author of *The Politics of School Desegregation* (1969, Doubleday) and co-author of five books, including *Making School Desegregation Work* (Ballinger) and *Stepping Over the Colorline: Black Inner-City Students in White Suburban Schools* (in press, Yale University Press).

SUSAN E. EATON is assistant director of the Harvard Project on School Desegregation and a doctoral candidate at the Harvard Graduate School of Education. She has been the education writer for daily metropolitan newspapers in Massachusetts and Connecticut. She is co-author, with Gary Orfield, of *Dismantling Desegregation: The Quiet Reversal of Brown v. Board of Education*, to be published by the New Press in 1996.

RICHARD FOSSEY is associate professor of education law and policy at Louisiana State University. He received his doctorate in education policy from Harvard University and his law degree from the University of Texas School of Law. Prior to beginning an academic career, he practiced education law in Alaska, where he represented school boards in Inuit, Athabaskan, and other Alaska Native communities. His research interests include education law, school choice, child abuse and neglect, and school reform. Fossey is co-author, along with Michael Clay Smith, of *Crime on Campus: Liability Issues and Campus Administration,* published by Oryx Press and the American Council on Education.

JOHN FREEMAN is a doctoral student and research assistant at Louisiana State University. A former high school social studies teacher and principal, his research interests are school effectiveness and improvement, as well as school law and finance. Freeman also served as Managing Editor for this volume.

ANTOINE M. GARIBALDI is vice president for Academic Affairs and professor of education at Xavier University. He is the author of ten books and monographs and more than 60 chapters and scholarly articles on black colleges and universities, African

American males, minority teacher recruitment and retention, and urban education issues. Some of his recent books are: *The Education of African Americans* (co-edited with Charles Willie and Wornie L. Reed, 1991); *Teacher Recruitment and Retention* (1989); *The Revitalization of Teacher Education Programs at Historically Black Colleges* (1989); *Educating Black Male Youth: A Moral and Civic Imperative* (1988); and, *Black Colleges and Universities: Challenges for the Future* (1984). He received his undergraduate degree magna cum laude from Howard University in 1973 and his Ph.D. in Educational and Social Psychology from the University of Minnesota in 1976.

JIM GARVIN is an assistant professor of educational administration in the Department of Administrative and Foundational Services at Louisiana State University. His primary research interests include schools and communities, urban education, and sociology of education.

CHARLES L. GLENN is professor and chairman of the Department of Administration, Training, and Policy Studies in the Boston University School of Education. Previously he served 21 years as the Massachusetts official responsible for urban education and civil rights in schools, in which capacity he had primary responsibility for requiring and helping 16 cities to implement school desegregation plans. He has published three books and dozens of book chapters on equity issues, urban school reform, parental choice of schools, the education of immigrant and language-minority children and the accommodation of religious conviction in educational systems. Glenn has also been involved extensively with education policy issues in Western and Eastern Europe and has served as a consultant on equity issues to a number of states and large cities.

CHERYL BROWN HENDERSON is one of the daughters of the late Rev. Oliver Brown who was lead plaintiff in the landmark U.S. Supreme Court Case of 1954 — *Oliver L. Brown et al. v. The Board of Education of Topeka*. She has been an educator for 23 years in the positions of public school teacher, guidance counselor, university guest lecturer, and state administrator. She is currently Executive Director of the Brown Foundation for Educational Equity, Excellence, and Research, and co-owner of Brown &

Brown Associates educational consultants. Her recent published writing is an article entitled "Landmark Decision: Remembering the Struggle for Equal Education," *Land and People, 6*(1), Spring 1994.

FREDERICK S. HUMPHRIES has served as a university president for more than twenty years, including 10 years at the helm of Tennessee State University and more than a decade as president of Florida A & M University. He became FAMUs eighth president in 1985 and has since earned national acclaim for his achievements, which helped FAMU become one of the nation's premier institutions of higher learning. In 1992, FAMU became the first university to defeat Harvard University in the recruitment of National Achievement Scholars, the most highly recruited African American scholars in the nation. One of the nation's most honored educators, Humphries serves on numerous boards of distinction in the private and public sectors. He is a 1957 magna cum laude graduate of FAMU with a bachelor's degree in chemistry and a Ph.D. in physical chemistry from the University of Pittsburgh in 1964.

JACQULIN SENSLEY JACOBS earned her doctorate from George Peabody College of Vanderbilt University and is currently employed at Southern University in Baton Rouge. Dr. Jacobs's professional career has been focused on researching, teaching, and informing the educational community about the academic and social needs of children that are culturally different. She has published book chapters, articles in scholarly journals, and made numerous presentations at national conferences on learning styles, multicultural education, test-taking skills, and techniques that work with culturally different children.

SHARON R. JOHNSON is currently the Writing/Reading/Study Skills Component Coordinator of the Thomas J. Edwards Learning Center located at the State University of New York at Buffalo. She is completing her doctoral dissertation in the Department of Education, Organization, Administration, and Policy at the State University of New York at Buffalo. Her research focuses on school desegregation and its legal and social impact on the quality of education for African American children.

KOFI LOMOTEY is chair and an associate professor in the Department of Administrative and Foundational Services in the College of Education at Louisiana State University in Baton Rouge. His research interests include African American principals, independent African-centered schools, issues of race in higher education, and urban education. His recent publications include "African-American Principals: Bureaucrat/Administrators and Ethno-humanists," in M. J. Shujaa (Ed.), *Too Much Schooling, Too Little Education: A Paradox in African-American Life* (1994) and "Social and Cultural Influences on Schooling: A Commentary on the UCEA Knowledge Base Project, Domain I, in *Educational Administration Quarterly, 31*(2) (1995). Lomotey is the editor of the journal *Urban Education* and the National Secretary/Treasurer of the Council of Independent Black Institutions, an umbrella organization for independent African-centered schools. In addition, he serves on the editorial boards of several journals, including *Educational Administration Quarterly* and *Journal for a Just and Caring Education.*

JAMES MEZA, JR. is director of the Accelerated Schools Center and associate professor of educational administration at the University of New Orleans in New Orleans. He served six years as a member of the Southern University System Board of Supervisors and chairperson of the Southern System's Academic Affairs, Faculty, and Personnel Committee. He also served as executive director of the Louisiana State Board of Elementary and Secondary Education.

GARY A. ORFIELD is professor of education, at the Harvard Graduate School of Education. His primary research interests are government policy and minority opportunity. He is co-author, with Susan Eaton, of *Dismantling Desegregation: The Quiet Reversal of Brown v. Board of Education*, to be published by the New Press in 1996.

SHARIBA RIVERS is a graduate student at Louisiana State University in the Department of Administrative and Foundational Services. She is currently working on her Master's Degree with a concentration in Higher Education Administration and serves as a graduate/research assistant for Dr. Kofi Lomotey.

JANET WARD SCHOFIELD is professor of psychology and a senior scientist in the Learning Research and Development Center at the University of Pittsburgh. She has also served as a faculty member at Spelman College. She received a B.A. magna cum laude from Radcliffe College where she was elected to Phi Beta Kappa. She received her Ph.D. from Harvard University in 1972. Professor Schofield is a social psychologist whose major research interest for more than twenty years has been social processes in desegregated schools. She has published more than two dozen papers in this area as well as two books. One of these, *Black and White in School: Trust, Tension or Tolerance?* was awarded the Society for the Psychological Study of Social Issues' Gordon Allport Intergroup Relations Prize.

MWALIMU J. SHUJAA is an associate professor in the area of social and philosophical foundations of education at the State University of New York at Buffalo. The focus of his academic research and writing is in the areas of theory and practice that add clarity to our understandings of (1) the social and cultural tensions that affect schooling and education; (2) the right of all people to cultural and political self-determination; and (3) the complexities of the personal transformations involved in liberating African consciousness from white supremacy ideology. Shujaa's edited book, *Too Much Schooling, Too Little Education: A Paradox of Black Life and White Societies* (published by Africa World Press, 1994), is an attempt to expand the conceptual bases for differentiating schooling and education in societies where the relationships of power between cultural groups are unequal and antagonistic. A second edited book, *Beyond Desegregation: The Politics of Quality in African American Schooling* (published by Corwin Press, 1996), examines the power relations affecting the schooling of people of African descent in the United States. He is also the editor of the journal *Education Policy*, and has been an Executive Officer of the Council of Independent Black Institutions since 1990.

DELORES R. SPIKES is president of the Southern University A & M College System and was directly involved in Louisiana's higher education desegregation case since 1981. She is past chairperson of Council 1890 Presidents, National Association of State Universities and Land Grant Colleges and currently serves as a Commissioner for the Southern Association of Colleges and Schools. She is a member of President Clinton's Advisory Board for Historically Black Universities and ACE/AID representative, University of Northwest in MMabatho, South Africa.

JOHN H. STANFIELD is professor of sociology and professor of African American and African Studies, University of California – Davis.

WILLIAM F. TATE is an assistant professor of curriculum and instruction at the University of Wisconsin–Madison. His research interests include the political and cultural dimensions of mathematics education. "School Mathematics and African American Students: Thinking Seriously About Opportunity-to-Learn Standadds," to appear in *Educational Administration Quarterly*, reflects his scholarly interests.

CHARLES TEDDLIE is professor of educational research methodology in the College of Education at Louisiana State University. He also taught at the University of New Orleans and served as Assistant Superintendent for Research and Development at the Louisiana Department of Education. He has published over 60 chapters and articles and co-authored two recent books: *Schools Make a Difference: Lessons Learned from a 10-year Study of School Effects* (1993, Teachers College Press) and *Advances in School Effectiveness Research and Practice* (1994, Pergamon). He serves as the series editor for *Readings on Equal Education, Volumes 13-17*. He received his B.S. cum laude in Psychology from LSU and his M.A. and Ph.D. (1979) from the University of North Carolina in Social Psychology.

J. DALE THORN is assistant professor of mass communications at Louisiana State University in Baton Rouge. A former associate commissioner of higher education in Louisiana, he has written a number of articles on higher education desegregation. He presented a paper on the topic at the 1994 National Conference on Race Relations and Civil Rights, at the Roy Wilkins Center, University of Minnesota. He is indebted to the Freedom Forum Foundation and the LSU Research Council for grants that supported this research.

JEROLD WALTMAN is professor of political science at the University of Southern Mississippi. He is the author of several books, the most recent of which is *American Government: Politics and Citizenship* (1993). He is currently working on a history of the minimum wage.

AMY STUART WELLS is an assistant professor of educational policy at UCLAs Graduate School of Education and Information Studies. Her areas of research include school desegregation, school choice policy, and detracking in racially mixed schools. She is author of *Time to Choose: America at the Crossroads of School Choice Policy* (1993, Hill & Wang) and co-author with Robert L. Crain of *Stepping Over the Colorline: Black Inner-City Students in White Suburban Schools* (in press, Yale University Press).

REGINALD WILSON was named Senior Scholar of the American Council on Education in October, 1988. He joined the Council as Director of the Office of Minority Concerns on October 1, 1981. Prior to that appointment he was, for nearly ten years, President of Wayne County Community College in Detroit. Dr. Wilson is the co-author of *Human Development in the Urban Community*, the editor of *Race and Equity in Higher Education*, and the author of *Civil Liberties and the U.S.* He is also on the editorial board of *The American Journal of Education* and *The Urban Review*.

CHAPTER 12

SOCIAL AND CULTURAL EFFECTS
OF SCHOOL DESEGREGATION:
AN INTRODUCTORY OVERVIEW

Kofi Lomotey and Charles Teddlie

Section II, Social and Cultural Effects of School Desegregation, contains five rather diverse chapters reviewing the impact of
the *Brown* decision on different aspects of the U.S. social and
cultural scene. These diverse components include educational
reform (especially in mathematics), urban schooling, the long-term
effects of schooling on the "life chances" of African Americans,
housing patterns for African Americans, and news media coverage
of desegregation cases.

A common theme running through four of these five chapters
(all except Chapter Fourteen by Wells and Cain) is that of
pessimism. The authors of these chapters argue that the *Brown*
decision has *not* had the desired impact on several important social
and cultural dimensions of the country.

The authors of two of these chapters were consciously writing
either from the perspective of critical race theory (Tate in Chapter
Thirteen) or the perspective of "race as a socialization agent"
(Stanfield in Chapter Sixteen). For both these authors, the impact
of the *Brown* decision has necessarily been limited, because of the

inherent nature of race relations in the U.S., which can be explained either in terms of the "structural inequality of capitalism" (Tate) or "normative white domination" (Stanfield). Tate illustrates one of his points by referring to D. A. Bell's insightful analysis that a "serious limitation of traditional civil rights legislation is that it is built on appeals to human rights in a society based on property rights."

The other two chapters with somewhat pessimistic assessments are concerned with housing patterns (Garvin in Chapter Fifteen), and news media "myopia" in the coverage of desegregation issues (Thorn in Chapter Seventeen). While not necessarily written from a "race-centered" perspective, these two chapters also discuss societal forces that have mitigated against the potentially salubrious effects of *Brown*: the use of social power by those who have traditionally possessed it, or a news media that is more concerned with sound bites than with the complex (and often hard to understand) issues that surround desegregation.

We now turn to more specific points from each of the chapters in this section. William Tate examines the political philosophy guiding the school mathematics experiences of African American students in the post-*Brown* era in Chapter Thirteen. According to him, the *Brown* decision has served as a symbol of economic hope in the African American community for over 40 years. He therefore advocates that it is extremely important to examine the relationship between mathematics — a subject closely connected to the economic well-being of individuals and society — and a law that has a 40–year connection to the economic interests of the African American community. He also suggests that the timing of the *Brown* decision and efforts to implement *Brown* coincided with the mathematics reform movement associated with Sputnik.

Tate concludes that advocates of African American education and, specifically, African American mathematics education, should be careful about adapting political philosophy associated with global competition because such a perspective is associated with a world view that fails to consider the history and realities of the African American experience. He further suggests that we seek to "eradicate artifacts of segregation such as ability grouping, tracking, and lack of fiscal support."

For the last 30 years, the bulk of research on school desegregation has focused on the short-term effects of this policy on the achievement, self-esteem, and intergroup relations of students in racially mixed versus segregated schools. These research foci reflect a more psychological approach to understanding the goals and purposes of school desegregation, viewing it as a policy designed to save the "hearts and minds" of African American students and teach children of all races to get along.

Chapter Fourteen brings together, for the first time, a smaller body of literature on the long-term effects of school desegregation on the life chances of African American students. In this chapter, Wells and Crain argue from a sociological perspective that the goal of desegregation policy is to break the cycle of segregation and allow African America and Hispanic students access to high-status institutions and the powerful social networks within them. They analyze 21 studies drawing on perpetuation theory, a macro-micro theory of racial segregation.

Jim Garvin argues that although the 1954 *Brown* decision was intended to enable education to become the arbiter of social change for this country, some 40 years later, education is nothing more than a reflection of the use of social power and how that power determines social place. In Chapter Fifteen, he examines the social impact of public housing and urban school systems to determine the effects of the *Brown* decision. He concludes that the results are not encouraging. According to Garvin, 40 years after the *Brown* decision, the social context of where and how people live has a severe impact on where and how they are schooled, what they are taught, and demonstrates who has power and who does not.

In Chapter Sixteen, John Stanfield takes a look at the issues surrounding urban school desegregation. He begins by suggesting that the U.S. is a "race-centered nation in which race serves as a continuous powerful socialization agency on everyday levels as well as on attitudinal and blatant attitudinal levels." He further notes that it would be absurd to assume that schools and educational processes can be divorced from such a system. According to Stanfield, although there are some school administrators, teachers, parents, and students who have worked in unison to create and maintain schools with positive multiethnic learning environments, there are also cases in which such efforts continue to be met with resistance efforts on the part of states, local governments, media, political parties, and organized citizen groups.

To address the challenges of urban school desegregation more effectively, Stanfield recommends the formation of citizen advocacy groups and coalitions across ethnic lines with other people of color both within communities and across the country. But before that happens, he cautions that African Americans must become clear about what they want out of enrolling their children in desegregated schools: desegregation, assimilation, pluralism, or some combination.

J. Dale Thorn examines the "mediocrity" of the media coverage of higher education desegregation issues during what he calls "the Second Reconstruction." Thorn comments, in Chapter Seventeen, that the coverage and commentary of even the prestige press in the early years of desegregation cases was marked by inaccuracy and distortion. He makes this point by identifying several instances in which journalists failed to tell the full story of court proceedings, ignored an appellate hearing in a case from a neighboring state and failed to interview or profile African American plaintiffs. He further notes that since newspapers have been allowed to go where cameras and recorders cannot (e.g., the federal courts), the printed press must accept much of the responsibility for the public's confusion about higher education desegregation cases.

Thorn's chapter more completely addresses a theme earlier discussed in Chapter Two — the cleavage that developed between the NAACP and the administrations at HBCUs over the desegregation of these institutions. He analyzes the media's lack of coverage of this important issue and their subsequent failure to report on the NAACP's apparent change with regard to policy on higher education desegregation that emerged during the Mississippi case. During this case, members of the NAACP protested *against* the threatened closures/mergers of HBCUs in Mississippi.

CHAPTER 13

BROWN, SPUTNIK, AND MATHEMATICS REFORM: LESSONS FROM THE PAST

William F. Tate

More than 40 years have passed since the historic *Brown* decision and African Americans continue to experience segregated and inequitable schooling. One explanation for the continuation of inequitable schooling lies in the restrictive vision of anti-discrimination law imposed by the Supreme Court (Crenshaw, 1988; Tate, Ladson-Billings, & Grant, 1993). This restrictive interpretation of achieving equality, not equity, emphasized process and minimized the significance of actual outcomes. This was evident in *Brown v. Board of Education* (1955, hereafter *Brown II*). The Supreme Court failed to give a description of the intended outcome of the decision. Instead, it transferred authority for elucidating, assessing, and solving the problem to school authorities. The role of the courts was relegated to monitoring the process of school desegregation. This restrictive role has enabled many school districts to devise educational programs that appear to constitute "good faith" implementation efforts, but that are instead educationally bankrupt.

For example, the Miami and Houston school districts counted Hispanic Americans as white and bused low-income African American children into low-income Hispanic American schools and vice versa (Orfield, 1988). This practice was not problematic

251

for policymakers seeking equality. However, the practice resulted in inequitable resource distributions. Another example is the segregation of school mathematics courses within school systems that have otherwise complied with court orders to desegregate faculty, school buildings, and other components of a school system (Donelan, Neal, & Jones, 1994; Oakes, 1985). These educational practices may have been avoided if the Supreme Court had provided a more expansive interpretation of the law that sought to achieve equity rather than numerical equality.

In contrast to the restrictive vision, an expansive vision of anti-discrimination law stresses equity and social justice. This interpretation of law looks to eliminate conditions of African American subordination and uses the power of the legal system to eradicate racial injustice. For too long equality and equity have been used interchangeably. Policies focused on equality are group-based and quantitative. The search for equal education is inappropriate because it assumes different groups of people need exactly the same treatment. In contrast, policies designed to achieve equity can be applied to groups or individuals; they are qualitative in that equity is linked to notions of social justice (Secada, 1991).

Instrumental in the construction of more expansive conceptions of equity is the scholarship of critical race theorists (e.g., Bell, 1992; Crenshaw, 1988; Delgado, 1990; Matsuda, 1989; Williams, 1991), which to date have been labeled as too radical and/or anti-democratic.[1] The purpose of this chapter is to explicate this line of thinking and use it as an analytic tool for understanding the political philosophy guiding the school mathematics experiences of African American students in the post-*Brown* era.

My reason for examining the political philosophy guiding the opportunities for African American children to learn mathematics in the post-*Brown* era is twofold. First, the *Brown* decision has served as a symbol of economic hope in the African American community for over 40 years. Thus, it is extremely important to examine the relationship between mathematics, a subject closely

---

[1] The character assassination of President Clinton's Civil Rights Commission nominee, Lani Guinier, by the press and politicians (Republicans and Democrats, alike) illustrates the fear and intolerance of dialogue built on the critical race theoretical perspective.

connected to the economic well-being of individuals and society, and a law that has a 40-year connection to the economic interests of the African American community. Second, the timing of the *Brown* decision and efforts to implement *Brown* coincided with the mathematics reform movement associated with Sputnik.

This chapter revisits the "*Brown*-Sputnik era," and examines the philosophical tenets undergirding federal policy in both reform efforts. The next section describes the theoretical lens used in my analysis.

The Need for a Critical Race Perspective

The need for a critical race analysis is precipitated by the reality that among constructs of "difference," race remains untheorized.[2] Despite the ground-breaking scholarship of DuBois (1919) and Woodson (1933/1990), many scholars have continued to use race as a variable to compare and contrast social conditions, rather than as a central theoretical and analytical tool. Unlike race, both gender and class have transcended the narrow limitation of being the "object" of scientific manipulation and have been recognized as the "subjects" of study. In the case of gender, feminist theories have been delineated and debated (e.g., Chodorow, 1978; DeBouvoir, 1961; Hartsock, 1979). Similarly, class analyses frame many explanations of social inequality (e.g., Apple, 1979; Bowles & Gintis, 1976; Carnoy, 1974). Despite its centrality in negotiating and understanding the social folkways of the U.S., race continues to be a silent, yet central construct in the "American Experience" (Giovanni, 1994; Lawrence-Lightfoot, 1994; Takaki, 1993).

In response to this silence, critical race scholars have begun to examine the underlying philosophies of traditional civil rights legislation for its ability to address the racism experienced by people of color (Crenshaw, 1988). Rather than a direct attack on civil rights legislation (a common conservative strategy), this scholarship attempts to understand it, build upon it, and propose different legal solutions. A serious limitation of traditional civil rights legislation is that it is built on appeals to human rights in a society based on property rights (Bell, 1987, 1992). Some dis-

---

[2] Omi and Winant (1994) argued that theories related to race fail to disentangle race and ethnicity or race and class, which is exactly my point.

cussions of democracy conflate it with capitalism despite the fact that it is possible to have a democratic government without capitalism (Marable, 1983). Discussing capitalism and democracy as if they were the same disguises the impact of capitalism on those who are relegated to its lowest economic ranks. More traditional civil rights approaches to solving injustice have depended on the "rightness" of democracy while disregarding the structural inequality of capitalism (Allen, 1974; Bell, 1987, 1992). However, democracy in the U.S. is difficult to separate from the workings of capitalism (Smith, 1937).

Similarly, school mathematics is closely associated with the workings of capitalism. Many advocates of school mathematics reform and equity have argued that African American students warrant better mathematics education on the grounds of national economic interest and global competition (Secada, 1991). For example, a report from the Mid-Atlantic Equity Center (1992) stated:

> When considering issues related to minority group under participation in science and mathematics, national and international contexts must be recognized. With the now emerging global economy, our nation's businesses beg for technologically literate workers, while at the same time, the National Science Foundation projects a shortage of over a million scientists and engineers by 2010 . . . . The widely publicized reform movements currently underway in pre-college mathematics and science education are unquestionably intended to address this national crisis which crosses race, socioeconomic, gender, and cultural lines. (pp. 4–5)

The realities of race and mathematics education have been converted into a rhetoric of global competition where racism and structural inequality receive little or no attention. History provides important lessons about the impact of educational policies built upon precepts of global competition with little attention paid to achieving equity.

Lessons From the Past: *Brown* and Sputnik

The purpose of this section is to examine the philosophical arguments put forth by policymakers in support of *Brown* and the mathematics reform movement that followed the launching of Sputnik. At the height of the McCarthy era, when members of

Congress were concerned with communist expansion in American life, the Supreme Court upheld loyalty oath requirements, and President Truman was actively engaged in removing alleged communists in government, while the U.S. Attorney General filed a pro-civil rights brief supporting *Brown* (Dudziak, 1988). This support was at odds with the restrictive approach to individual rights that was prevalent at the time (Allen, 1974). However, the U.S. government's participation in the desegregation case during the McCarthy era was no accident. It was driven by America's political ideology. Moreover, the American political ideology of the time provides insight into the similarities and contradictions of *Brown* and the Sputnik-driven mathematics reform movement.

The Rationale for *Brown*

In an article in the NAACP's December 1935 *Crisis*, "Don't Shout Too Soon," Charles Houston remarked: "Lawsuits mean little unless supported by public opinion. Nobody needs to explain to the Negro the difference between the law in books and the law in action" (Davis & Clark, 1992, p. 89). Houston's caution followed a NAACP victory in the lawsuit *Pearson v. Murray* (1936). Houston warned that court victories did not guarantee social change. The spirit of Houston's remark was articulated 45 years later by Derrick Bell in his analysis examining the rationale for *Brown*. Bell (1980) stated:

> The interests of Blacks in achieving racial equality will be accommodated only when it converges with the interests of Whites; however, the fourteenth amendment, standing alone, will not authorize a judicial remedy providing effective racial equality for Blacks where the remedy sought threatens the superior societal status of middle- and upper-class Whites. (p. 95)

Bell (1980) noted that the issue of school segregation and the harm it inflicted on African American children had been a part of legal discourse for over 100 years at the time of the *Brown* decision. Yet, prior to *Brown*, the claim of harm from segregated public schools had been met with orders to "equalize" facilities. Bell (1980) raised the question, "What accounted, then, for the sudden shift in 1954 away from the separate but equal doctrine and towards a commitment to desegregation" (p. 96). Bell (1980) contended that the break from the Supreme Court's long held position cannot be understood without considering the position of whites, not just those whites concerned about the immorality of racial injustice, but those whites in policymaking positions able to see the economic and political advantages of abandoning segregation. Bell offered three reasons for outlawing school segregation that converged with white economic self-interest.

First, Bell (1980) argued that the *Brown* decision helped the U.S. in its struggle to minimize the spread of communist philosophy to third world nations. In many countries, the credibility of the United States had been damaged by the inequitable social conditions (e.g., segregation) that existed. Both the NAACP and government lawyers argued the *Brown* decision would help legitimize the political and economic philosophies of the United States with third world nations (Bell, 1980).

Similarly, Dudziak (1988) reported that federal policy on civil rights during the Truman Administration was framed with the international implications of U.S. race relations in mind. Moreover, through a series of amicus briefs describing the potential impact of racial segregation on U.S. foreign policy interests, the Administration impressed upon the Supreme Court the connection between national security, economic growth, and upholding civil rights at home.

Second, Bell (1980) contended that *Brown* provided reassurance to African Americans that the struggle for freedom and equality fought for during World War II might become a reality at home (Bell, 1980; Takaki, 1993). African American veterans faced not only racial inequality, but were also subjected to violent beatings in the South. In response, one African American leader, Paul Robeson argued:

> It is unthinkable . . . that American Negroes would go to war on behalf of those who have oppressed us for generations . . . against a country [the Soviet Union] which in one generation has raised our people to the full human dignity of mankind. (Foner, 1978, pp. 17–18)

According to Bell (1980), it is reasonable to assume that those in control of America would recognize the importance of negating the dialogue of Robeson and others with similar views. Robeson's perspective was an affront to the national interest. Thus, racial decisions by the courts were pivotal to softening criticism about the contradiction of a free and just America (Dudziak, 1988).

Finally, there were white capitalists who understood that the South could not be transformed from an agrarian society to the more industrialized Sunbelt under the cloud of divisive battles over state-supported segregation (Allen, 1974; Bell, 1980; Heilbroner, 1968; Marable, 1983). In essence, segregation was a barrier obstructing the economic and property interests of white profit-makers.

These reasons may seem insufficient proof of the national economic interest leveraged to influence a Supreme Court decision as important as *Brown*. In fact, as with the abolition of slavery, there were whites who viewed racial justice as sufficient motivation for change. However, like the abolition movement, the number of whites who would act on moral reasoning alone was not sufficient to catalyze the changes necessary for racial reform.

Sputnik: Global Competition and Gifted Education

In 1957, two years after *Brown II*, the Soviet Union launched Sputnik, the world's first earth-orbiting satellite. The general consensus among the U.S. mass media was that Soviet technological success was attributable to their school system. In contrast, the 1950s brought criticism of the U.S. educational system, more specifically mathematics education, from officials of industry, colleges and universities, and the military. According to Kleibard (1987):

> Just as Prussian schools were widely believed to be the basis for the victory of the Prussians over the Austrians in the Battle of Konigratz in 1866, so, implausibly, did the Soviet technological feat become a victory of the Soviet educational system over the American. (p. 265)

The media reported that Soviet children were immersed in the hard sciences and mathematics required for the global competition that was the heart of the Cold War.

The shock of Sputnik sparked the movement to improve mathematics education in the United States, for it was thought that only through scientific education could the American dream be realized and preserved. Moreover, this mathematics reform effort was connected to the political climate of the times. Devault and Weaver (1970) stated:

> Indeed, one wonders if the reform movement would have been as successful and would have received such substantial financial support if the event of Sputnik had

not been preceded by the McCarthy era. Albeit an un-
healthy force in American political life, McCarthyism
led to an attitude that made arguments for funds for
education more attractive to legislators and the American life. (p. 267)

Who benefitted from the reform movement? Most efforts to
improve mathematics education were focused on the college-
bound student (Devault & Weaver, 1970). The decision to focus
on college-bound students reflected the tension between calls for
school equality and educational policies designed to address global
competition. The political philosophy undergirding mathematics
education reform was to invest resources in the students who were
perceived as America's best and brightest. Thus, notions of
achieving equity were often seen as misguided. For example, Vice
Admiral Hyman G. Rickover, who was credited with the development of the atomic submarine, contended that American education
had gone "soft" (Kleibard, 1987). Rickover had acquired a reputation as an intellectual and carried influence with many members
of Congress. He used this influence to deliver the message that a
misconceived interpretation of equality had led American schools
astray. Rickover argued that the gifted and talented of the country
were neglected. He and others such as the College Entrance Examination Board's Commission on Mathematics and the National
Council of Teachers of Mathematics Secondary-School Curriculum Committee sought to restrict mathematics reform efforts to
"college-capable" students (Devault & Weaver, 1970; Kleibard,
1987; National Council of Teachers of Mathematics [NCTM],
1959).

The appeal to limit the mathematics reform effort to gifted
and talented students was built upon a political philosophy that
sought to protect the national interest. Similarly, the philosophy
undergirding the *Brown* decision was associated with efforts to
protect the economic interests of the nation. Despite this similar-
ity, the mathematics reform generated as a result of Sputnik was
closely connected to an elitist philosophy that worked at odds with
efforts to establish equal educational opportunities for African
American students.

The Sputnik reform missed the mark.

The impact of limiting the mathematics reform effort to
talented and gifted students was not beneficial to most African

American students. Perhaps an example will illustrate this point. During the 1953–54 school year, two educational funds collaborated in order to conduct a Southern talent search among the African American seniors of 81 segregated high schools of the region's 45 leading cities (Plant, 1957). During that academic year and the year that followed, 3,178 seniors who ranked in the upper 10% of the classes of these schools were assessed through a modified version of the Scholastic Aptitude Test of the College Entrance Examination Board. The test results revealed that more than half of these seniors made at least the minimum qualifying score set by the educational funds as the lowest possible indicator of success in higher education. The qualifying score was set at 600 (verbal and math sections combined) with the verbal section given twice the weight. However, when measured against the scores of all public school students, the 1,461 African American seniors tested in May 1953 averaged below the 78th percentile in verbal aptitude and the 66th percentile in mathematical. Very few of this elite group of African American students could be classified as gifted mathematically using this measurement system. Thus, we see that very few of the highest achieving African American students would have benefitted from mathematics reform efforts targeted for gifted students.

I am not suggesting African American students lacked the potential to do mathematics. Rather, the opportunity to learn more advanced levels of mathematics was limited by inadequate educational experiences. Woodson (1933/1990) described the school mathematics experience of many African American students:

> And even in the certitude of science and mathematics it has been unfortunate that the approach to the Negro has been borrowed from a "foreign" method. For example, the teaching of arithmetic in the fifth grade in a backward county in Mississippi should mean one thing in the Negro school and a decidedly different thing in the white school. The Negro children, as a rule, come from the homes of tenants and peons who have to migrate annually from plantation to plantation, looking for light which they have never seen. The children from the homes of white planters and merchants live permanently in the midst of calculations, family budgets, and the like, which enable them sometimes to learn more by contact

than the Negro can acquire in school. Instead of teaching such Negro children less arithmetic, they should be
taught much more of it than the white children, for the
latter attend a graded school consolidated by free transportation when the Negroes go to one-room hovels to be
taught without equipment and by incompetent teachers
educated scarcely beyond the eighth grade. (p. 4)

Woodson's (1933/1990) philosophical discussion of the
African American education condition and his conjecture about
improving student performance have been supported with empirical methods. Margo's (1990) econometric analyses of Southern
schools in the pre-*Brown* era found that, had African American
and white schools been "equal," African American children would
have attended school more frequently than they actually did.
Moreover, African American literacy rates and standardized test
scores would have been higher.

Woodson's and Margo's analyses imply that federal policy
supporting school mathematics programs only for the gifted — a
tacit form of school segregation — would impede the mathematics
achievement for African American students. History confirms this
implication.

The Ancestor of a Restrictive Vision: Tracking

The *Brown* decision was built upon a notion of equality that
equated school desegregation with equal protection under the law.
This restrictive view of equality evolved from pre-*Brown* litigation
in the area of education and related cases (e.g., *Plessy v. Ferguson*,
1896; *Missouri ex. rel Gaines v. Canada*, 1938; *McLaurin v.
Oklahoma State Regents for Higher Education*, 1950; *Sweatt v.
Painter*, 1950). On the basis of these precedents, the *Brown* decision resulted, and transformed the relations between African
Americans and whites in a variety of social contexts. This is an
important legacy of the *Brown* decision. However, in mathematics
education, *Brown* did not address or anticipate the political
influences on educators to construct racially segregated school
mathematics experiences known as ability groups or tracks.

Typically, ability grouping is associated with elementary
school mathematics, and tracks are products of secondary mathematics education (Oakes, 1985). However, both are sorting
practices that often result in racially segregated mathematics
experiences and lower mathematics achievement (Oakes, 1990;

Wheelock, 1992). The detection of both sorting practices is sometimes difficult. Donelan, Neal, and Jones (1994) stated:

> Tracking and ability grouping involve a variety of policy and placement procedures. While most primary schools rely upon within-class grouping, some offer pull-out sections for the gifted or the learning disabled. Some middle schools classify students by ability so that their entire schedule of classes can be determined; others sort students according to subject matter. Additionally, some schools have only two tracks (regular and college preparatory), while others have several (basic, average, enriched, honors, advanced placement, etc.). The lack of homogeneity in what constitutes tracking explains the confusion and polarities in the literature. (p. 378)

What is clear from the literature on tracking is that it impedes academic progress in school mathematics for many children. Students placed in lower tracks are exposed to limited, basic skills mathematics curriculum and ultimately achieve less than students of similar aptitude who are provided the opportunity to learn in more rigorous mathematics programs or untracked classes (Gamoran & Mare, 1989; Oakes, 1985, 1990). Teacher interaction with students in lower-track classes is less engaging and less supportive. Further, the teachers in the lower track classes are less demanding of higher-order thinking and of student contributions to classroom discussions (Good & Brophy, 1987). These classroom interactions often lack academic rigor and more likely focus on managing behavior (Eckstrom & Villegas, 1991; Oakes, 1985).

How should the next generation of school policymaking address tracking? The answer to this question should be derived from lessons learned in *Brown*. Despite its importance, the *Brown* decision is the product of a restrictive view of equality. The restrictive view defines equality as a process and rarely takes into consider outcomes (e.g., tracking). Crenshaw (1988) stated the following about the restrictive view:

> "Wrongdoing," moreover, is seen primarily as isolated actions against individuals rather than as societal policy against an entire group. Nor does the restrictive view contemplate the courts playing a role in redressing harms from America's racist past, as opposed to merely policing society to eliminate a narrow set of proscribed discriminatory practices. Moreover, even when injus-

tice is found, efforts to redress it must be balanced
against, and limited by, competing interests. (p. 1342)
The restrictive view of equality associated with school
desegregation combined with the elitist philosophy guiding policy
in mathematics education have supported the action of school
districts that have looked to evade the notions of equity and social
justice that embody *Brown*. The time has come for a more
expansive vision that seeks to produce high mathematics achievement for African American students.

Expanding the Vision: Creating Opportunity to Learn
Past mathematics education reforms have targeted the
"gifted" and have largely ignored the children most in need of
increased educational opportunity. These reform efforts have been
closely associated with a Eurocentric philosophy of elitism and
social stratification that sought to build the economic power of
corporate entities (Ernest, 1991; Joseph, 1987). In an effort to
expand beyond this approach to reform, I would like to sketch out,
in broad strokes, two issues that should be included in a movement
to reform mathematics education for African American students.

The Need for Fiscal Adequacy
The *Brown* decision declared "separate but equal" schooling
was unconstitutional. However, in the 1990s our school finance
methods create schools that are not only separate but blatantly
unequal (Denbo, Grant, Jackson, & Williams, 1994; Kozol, 1991).
The inequitable distribution of resources plays a significant role in
the achievement opportunities of African American students.
For example, Ferguson (1991) presented evidence that the
single most important measurable cause of increased student
achievement was teacher expertise, measured by teacher performance on a statewide recertification exam, teacher experience, and
master's degree. Ferguson (1991) found that expenditure levels
make a difference in increasing student performance as they influence a school district's ability both to contract higher-quality
teachers and to maintain other instructional programs, such as
extracurricular activities. Other studies support Ferguson's findings.
A 1990 national evaluation of 8th-grade mathematics programs found a strong relationship between students' economic
status and the level of resources provided to their instructional

programs (Educational Testing Service [ETS], 1991). More than 80% of teachers in schools with middle- to upper-class students obtained all or most of the materials and resources they requested for instructional purposes. In contrast, only 41% of teachers in schools with the largest concentration of lower socioeconomic students received all or most of the instructional materials they requested (ETS, 1991). Most importantly, the students whose teachers reported having limited materials and resources had lower mathematics achievement than those whose teachers indicated their materials were adequate. A disproportionate number of the students in the former group are African American. This reality is compounded by the fact that African American students have less access to the best qualified mathematics teachers and fewer opportunities to use technology in their school mathematics program (National Science Board [NSB], 1991; Piller, 1992).

Most of the studies examining the role of fiscal support on student achievement were conducted before many states and local school districts adopted recent recommendations calling for new mathematics standards (NCTM, 1989, 1991, 1993). The call for new mathematics standards represents a philosophical shift in school mathematics from a basic skills approach to a constructivist, technology-driven vision of mathematics pedagogy. The fiscal support required to implement a basic skills mathematics program is low in comparison to these recent recommendations. These new mathematics standards will require many schools educating African American students to (a) improve teachers' mathematics qualifications, (b) upgrade instructional materials (e.g., textbooks, calculators, software, computer facilities, and science laboratories), (c) provide summer enrichment programs in mathematics, and (d) enhance the quality of the infrastructure (e.g., deteriorating buildings and classrooms) (Clune, 1993; Entwisle & Alexander, 1992; Kozol, 1991; NCTM, 1989). The need to provide fiscal support for mathematics reform is a paramount consideration in schools that prepare African American students.

We Must Address Woodson's Notion of Foreign Method
    More than 60 years ago, Carter G. Woodson argued that the method used to educate African American students in mathematics was foreign to them. Woodson (1933/1990) contended that the African American student should be provided with more mathematics than typically offered in schools. He suggested that many

African American students were not afforded the opportunity to learn and use mathematics in their daily lives.

Today, school mathematics programs that seek to prepare African American students for the variety of situations they are likely to face as adults are influenced by the philosophy undergirding mathematics reform. Like the *Brown*-Sputnik era, the current reform movement in mathematics education has been guided by philosophical discussions linked to global economic competition (Secada, 1991). These appeals to global competition represent attempts to persuade educators to compromise their beliefs about individual human rights because of economic property interests. Discussions centered around the need to prepare a competitive workforce in a global economy, while persuasive to voters, generally neglect the barriers facing African American students in many school settings. In fact, history suggests that appeals to global competition are likely to generate interest for exclusionary practices such as gifted mathematics education programs. Instead, I contend that African American students should be provided with more mathematics.

Elsewhere, I described my own 6th-grade mathematics program (Tate, 1994). In retrospect, my experience was consistent with Woodson's recommendations. I was provided three classes of mathematics instruction. One class was very traditional and used a typical textbook program. This class provided me with the skills required to perform well on standardized measures of achievement. The second class was different in that no tests were given, and we spent a great deal of time discussing algebraic and geometric concepts. The focus of the class was the development of communication skills using mathematical ideas. This experience prepared me for a career where communicating about mathematics is a very important skill. The third class consisted mainly of a series of technical projects — e.g., the development of a classroom phone system — that required applying a variety of mathematical principles. The third class nurtured a zeal for mathematics and science that remains to this date. It was critical because preparing for standardized tests in mathematics, however important for future opportunities, did not provoke much desire for continued study. In combination, the above practices represent one way to implement the recent recommendations from the National Council of Teachers of Mathematics (NCTM, 1989, 1991). Regardless of how a school system chooses to implement these recommendations, the result should be the same for most African American students — more opportunities to learn mathematics than are currently provided. That is, Woodson's recommendation must be implemented, if equity and social justice is to be realized.

Final Remarks

Philosophy does not make the world; it makes the world more understandable. For too long policymakers have been committed to a philosophy of mathematics reform that fails to address the sociopolitical realities of the African American school experience. The status of African American students in the society is a product of contradictions in U.S. political philosophy. Nowhere is this more obvious than the *Brown*-Sputnik era.

Both *Brown* and the mathematics reform effort catalyzed by Sputnik were driven by a political philosophy that sought to address the threat of communist expansion. However, *Brown* and the Sputnik mathematics reform worked at cross purposes. The lesson to be learned from this is clear. Advocates of African American education and, specifically, mathematics education, should be careful about adapting political philosophy associated with global competition. This philosophical perspective is associated with a world view that fails to take into consideration the history and realities of the African American experience.

Instead, we who are concerned with improving the African American experience in school mathematics should seek to eradicate artifacts of segregation such as ability grouping, tracking, and lack of fiscal support. The legacy of *Brown* depends on our ability to design and implement policy that reflects the realities of the African American school experience.

References

Allen, R. (1974). *Reluctant reformers: The impact of racism on American social reform movements.* Washington, DC: Howard University.

Apple, M. W. (1979). *Ideology and curriculum.* London: Routledge & Kegan Paul.

Bell, D. A. (1980). Brown and the interest-convergence dilemma. In D. A. Bell (Ed.), *New perspectives on school desegregation* (pp. 90–107). New York: Teachers College Press.

Bell, D. A. (1987). *And we are not saved: The elusive quest for racial justice*. New York: Basic Books.

Bell, D. A. (1992). *Faces at the bottom of the well: The permanence of racism*. New York: Basic Books.

Bowles, S., & Gintis, H. (1976). *Schooling in capitalist America*. New York: Basic Books.

Chodorow, N. (1978). *The reproduction of mothering*. Berkeley, CA: University of California Press.

Clune, W. H. (1993). The shift from equity to adequacy in school finance. *The World and I, 8*, 389–405.

Crenshaw, K. W. (1988). Race, reform and retrenchment: Transformation and legitimation in anti-discrimination law. *Harvard Law Review, 101*, 1331–1387.

Davis, M. D., & Clark, H. R. (1992). *Thurgood Marshall: Warrior at the bar, rebel on the bench*. New York: Birch Lane.

DeBouvoir, S. (1961). *The second sex*. New York: Bantam Books.

Delgado, R. (1988). Critical legal studies and the realities of race: Does the fundamental contradiction have a corollary? *Harvard Civil Rights-Civil Liberties Law Review, 23*, 407–413.

Delgado, R. (1990). When a story is just a story: Does voice really matter? *Virginia Law Review, 76*, 95–111.

Denbo, S., Grant, C., Jackson, S., & Williams, B. (1994). *Educate America: A call of equity in school reform*. Chevy Chase, MD: Mid-Atlantic Equity Consortium.

Devault, M. V., & Weaver, J. F. (1970). Forces and issues related to curriculum and instruction, K–6. In A. F. Coxford & P. S. Jones (Eds.), *A history of mathematics education in the United States and Canada* (pp. 92–152). Washington, DC: National Council of Teachers of Mathematics.

Donelan, R. W., Neal, G. A., & Jones, D. L. (1994). The promise of *Brown* and the reality of academic grouping: The tracks of my tears. *Journal of Negro Education, 63*, 376–387.

DuBois, W. E. B. (1919, reprinted in 1989). *The souls of black folks*. New York: Penguin Books.

Dudziak, M. L. (1988). Desegregation as a cold war imperative. *Stanford Law Review, 41*, 61–120.

Eckstrom, R., & Villegas, A. M. (1991). Ability grouping in middle grade mathematics: Process and consequences. *Research in Middle Level Education, 15*(1), 1–20.

Educational Testing Service. (1991). *The state of inequality: A policy information report.* Princeton, NJ: Author.

Entwisle, D. R., & Alexander, K. L. (1992). Summer setback: Race, poverty, school composition and mathematics achievement in the first two years of school. *American Sociological Review, 57,* 72–84.

Ernest, P. (1991). *The philosophy of mathematics education.* London: Falmer Press.

Ferguson, R. F. (1991). Paying for public education: New evidence on how and why money matters. *Harvard Journal on Legislation, 28,* 465–498.

Foner, P. (Ed.) (1978). *Paul Robeson speaks.* New York: Citadel Press.

Gamoran, A., & Mare, R. (1989). Secondary school tracking and educational inequality: Compensation, reinforcement or neutrality? *American Journal of Sociology, 94,* 1146–1183.

Giovanni, N. (1994). *Racism 101.* New York: William Morrow.

Good, T. L., & Brophy, J. (1987). *Looking into classrooms.* New York: Harper & Row.

Hartsock, N. (1979). Feminist theory and the development of revolutionary strategy. In Z. Einstein (Ed.), *Capitalist patriarch and the case for socialist feminism.* London and New York: Monthly Review Press.

Heilbroner, R. L. (1968). *The making of economic society.* Englewood Cliffs, NJ: Prentice-Hall.

Joseph, G. C. (1987). Foundations of Eurocentrism in mathematics. *Race and Class, 28,* 13–28.

Kleibard, H. M. (1987). *The struggle for the American curriculum 1893–1958.* New York: Routledge & Kegan Paul.

Kozol, J. (1991). *Savage inequalities: Children in America's schools.* New York: Crown.

Lawrence-Lightfoot, S. (1994). *I've known rivers: Lives of loss and liberation.* Reading, MA: Addison-Wesley.

Marable, M. (1983). *How capitalism underdeveloped black America.* Boston: South End.

Margo, R. T. (1990). *Race and schooling in the South, 1880–1950: An economic history.* Chicago: University of Chicago Press.

Matsuda, M. (1989). Public response to racist speech: Considering the victim's story. *Michigan Law Review, 87,* 2320–2381.

Mid-Atlantic Equity Center. (1992). *Opening up the mathematics and science filters: Our schools did it, so can yours!* Washington, DC: American University, Mid-Atlantic Equity Center.

National Council of Teachers of Mathematics. (1989). *Curriculum and evaluation standards for school mathematics.* Reston, VA: Author.

National Council of Teachers of Mathematics. (1991). *Profes sional standards for teaching mathematics.* Reston, VA: Author.

National Council of Teachers of Mathematics. (1993). *Assessment standards for school mathematics* (Working Draft). Reston, VA: Author.

National Council of Teachers of Mathematics Secondary-School Curriculum Committee. (1959). The secondary mathematics curriculum. *Mathematics Teachers, 52,* 389–417.

National Science Board. (1991). *Science & engineering indicators* (NSB 91–1). Washington DC: U.S. Government Printing Office.

Oakes, J. (1985). *Keeping track: How schools structure inequality.* New Haven, CT: Yale University Press.

Oakes, J. (1990). Opportunities, achievement, and choice: Women and minority students in science and mathematics. In C. B. Cazden (Ed.), *Review of research in education* (Vol 16, pp. 153–222). Washington, DC: American Educational Research Association.

Omi, M., & Winant, H. (1994). *Racial formation in the United States from the 1960s to the 1990s* (2nd ed.). New York: Routledge.

Orfield, G. (1988). School desegregation in the 1980s. *Equity and Choice, 4,* 25.

Piller, C. (1992). Separate realities. *MACWORLD, 9*(9), 218–231.

Plant, R. L. (1957). *Blueprint for talent searching.* New York: National Scholarship Fund and Fund for Negro Students.

Secada, W. G. (1991). Agenda setting, enlightened self-interest, and equity in mathematics education. *Peabody Journal of Education, 66*(2), 22–56.

Smith, A. (1937). *An inquiry into the nature and causes of the wealth of nations.* New York: Random House.

Takaki, R. (1993). *A different mirror: A history of multicultural America.* Boston: Little, Brown and Co.

Tate, W. F. (1994). From inner city to ivory tower: Does my voice matter in the academy? *Urban Education, 29,* 245–269.

Tate, W. F., Ladson-Billings, G., & Grant, C. A. (1993). The *Brown* decision revisited: Mathematizing social problems. *Educational Policy, 7,* 255–275.

Wheelock, A. (1992). *Crossing the tracks.* New York: The New Press.

Williams, P. J. (1991). *The alchemy of race and rights: Diary of a law professor.* Cambridge, MA: Harvard University Press.

Woodson, C. G. (1990). *The mis-education of the Negro* (originally published in 1933). Trenton, NJ: Africa World Press.

Table of Legal Cases

McLaurin v. Oklahoma State Regents for Higher Education, 339 U.S. 637 (1950).

Missouri ex. rel Gaines v. Canada, 305 U.S. 337 (1938).

Pearson v. Murray, 169 Md. 478, 182 Atl. 590 (1936).

Plessy v. Ferguson, 163 U.S. 537 (1896).

Sweatt v. Painter, 339 U.S. 629 (1950).

CHAPTER 14

PERPETUATION THEORY AND THE LONG-TERM EFFECTS OF SCHOOL DESEGREGATION

Amy Stuart Wells and Robert L. Crain

> Though there may be overwhelming evidence that schools have not equalized life chances . . . such equalization remains a criterion worth using in asking the value of school desegregation. The research question that arises directly from this criterion is whether the life chances of blacks who attend desegregated schools are significantly improved over those of comparable blacks who do not. Because there is ample evidence that test scores and grades in school do not explain much of the variance in later income or status . . . these latter results must be studied directly . . . . (Granovetter, 1986, p. 103)

Lawyers and civil rights advocates who presented constitutional and moral arguments for school desegregation believed that institutions would enhance their opportunities for social mobility

This chapter was originally published as "Perpetuation Theory and the Long-term Effects of School Desegregation" by A. S. Wells and R. L. Crain, 1994, *Review of Education Research, 60*(4), pp. 531–555. Copyright 1994 by the American Educational Research Association. Reprinted by permission.

and thus improve their life chances. The NAACP desegregation cases preceding the landmark *Brown* ruling were predicated on the theory that degrees from prestigious, predominantly white universities were the keys to high-status employment, social net-works, and social institutions. Without access to these universities and the status of the degrees they conferred, African Americans, no matter what their level of educational achievement or attainment, would remain a separate and unequal segment of our guaranteeing African Americans access to predominantly white society (Kluger, 1975). This is a structural argument aimed at addressing barriers to social mobility. Since the early 1950s, arguments for school desegregation have become more disparate as psychologists and educators have maintained that providing African American children with access to white educational institutions from which their parents had been excluded could potentially lead to several short-term outcomes: greater self-esteem, academic achievement, and educational attainment for African American students, and improved race relations among all students. Beginning with Kenneth and Mamie Clarks' research on African American children and dolls, the rationale for desegregating elementary and secondary school students has been more steeped in psychological theory about feelings of inferiority than in sociological theory of social structure and status attainment (Rosenberg, 1986). After the Coleman report of 1966, desegregation was given an additional social-psychological rationale: placing low-income African American students in schools and classrooms with middle-class white students would enhance their educational achievement by exposing them to better prepared and more motivated peers. "Despite the very contradictory literature on school desegregation, the case for desegregation was seen as hinging *primarily* on whether it improves the achievement test scores of minority students" (Levin, 1975, p. 238).

In part because of this shifting focus, and in part because policymakers require instant feedback, most school desegregation research conducted during the late 1960s and early 1970s focused on short-term effects — i.e., achievement test scores, intergroup relations, self-esteem of African American students, and levels of white flight (Braddock & McPartland, 1982; Levin, 1975). Meanwhile, policymakers and researchers lost sight of many of the original theoretical underpinnings embedded in the long-term goals of school desegregation policy. As Prager, Longshore, and

Seeman (1986) note, "desegregation research has suffered because it has come to stand as a kind of scholarship guided largely by public concerns and public issues, not by theoretically generated empirical questions" (p. 4).

In an attempt to refocus the debate on more theoretical and sociological arguments, we have drawn together 21 of the most substantial studies on the long-term effects of school desegregation. This body of literature remains significantly smaller than research on short-term effects, but it is more recent. Much of this work was published in the last 10 years as the long-term effects of desegregation plans implemented in the late 1960s and early 1970s became more apparent. Meanwhile, due to the ambiguous findings of the research on short-term effects and the ongoing resistance of many white Americans to desegregation policies, school desegregation had already been declared a failure in many policy circles by the time much of this literature on long-term effects was available. Thus, the more positive findings in these studies have been virtually ignored, and this is the first article to bring them together and examine them as a whole through the lens of perpetuation theory — a micro-macro sociological theory of racial segregation originally developed by Braddock (1980).

We believe that, in order to assess the impact of school desegregation policy on the status attainment of African American adults, researchers and policymakers need to look beyond the short-term effects, especially standardized test scores, and focus more on long-term social and economic outcomes. Because educational achievement alone does not solve the problem of economic inequality, school desegregation must do more than raise African American students' test scores; it must also break the cycle of racial segregation that leaves African Americans and whites worlds apart. This is not to say that equal educational outcomes for all students is unimportant, or that higher achievement levels for African American students should not be a national goal. But these outcomes do not necessarily hinge on the racial makeup of schools. African American children do not need to sit next to white children to learn, although they are more likely to have access to high-status knowledge if they do. Still, in our study of network analysis we are inspired by the old adage that *who you know* is as important (or even more important) in social mobility as *what you* know; we believe, therefore, that the lawyers and civil rights advocates of the 1940s and 1950s knew what they were talking about. The social network advantage of desegregated schools for African American students is real, even though it could not be measured in time to satisfy policymakers who have lost sight of the original goals of desegregation.

Theoretical Context

Perpetuation theory, as developed by Braddock (1980) and McPartland and Braddock (1981), states that segregation tends to repeat itself "across the stages of the life cycle and across institutions when individuals have not had sustained experiences in desegregated settings earlier in life" (McPartland & Braddock, 1981, p. 149). Drawing on Pettigrew's research on social inertia and avoidance learning, Braddock (1980) derived perpetuation theory by focusing on the tendency of African Americans to perpetuate racial segregation. He notes that minority students who have not regularly experienced the realities of desegregation may overestimate the degree of overt hostility they will encounter or underestimate their skill at coping with strains in interracial situations. These segregated students will, in most instances, make choices that maintain physical segregation when they become adults because they have never tested their racial beliefs. While Braddock's perpetuation theory does not preclude the existence of real structural constraints to racial desegregation, his focus is on how individual agents adjust their behavior to accommodate, and thus perpetuate, these constraints, and how exposure to desegregated settings can change this behavior.

We have expanded on Braddock's theory of perpetual segregation by considering it alongside network analysis, or the more structural argument that segregation is perpetuated across generations because African Americans and Hispanic Americans lack access to informal networks that provide information about, and entrance to, desegregated institutions and employment. This structural explanation of perpetual segregation complements Braddock's writing on African Americans' lack of information on which to test their racial beliefs. In applying network analysis to perpetuation theory, we draw from Granovetter's (1973, 1983, 1986) work, which shows the strong impact of "weak ties," or less formal interpersonal networks — that is, acquaintances or friends of friends — on the diffusion of influence, information, and mobility opportunities. These weak ties, Granovetter (1973) argues, are the channels through which ideas that are socially distant from an individual may reach him.

In linking his work to the research of Braddock and others who study the effects of school desegregation, Granovetter (1986) notes the importance of weak ties in bridging the often separate cliques of white and nonwhite teenagers. Desegregated schools may be the only institutions in which African American and Hispanic American students would have access to the abundance of college and employment contacts that white and wealthy students often take for granted:

> School desegregation studies frequently show that cross-racial ties formed are not very strong. But even such weak ties may significantly affect later economic success. Because employers at all levels of work prefer to recruit by word-of-mouth, typically using recommendations of current employees, segregation of friendship and acquaintance means that workplaces that start out all white will remain so. (Granovetter, 1986, p. 102–103)

Other network analysts have argued (i.e., Lin, 1990; Montgomery, 1992) that people on the bottom of the social structure, including African American students from low-income families, have more to gain than white and wealthy students from the use of weak ties because these ties will invariably link them to more affluent and better connected people, whereas strong ties usually connect them to family and close friends who are also poor. Lin and others have found that "the advantage of using weaker ties over the use of stronger ties decreases as the position of origin approaches the top of the hierarchy" (Lin, 1990, p. 251).

As Wilson (1987) and other social scientists have noted, the greatest barrier to social and economic mobility for inner city African Americans is the degree to which they remain isolated from the opportunities and networks of the mostly white and middle-class society. Hoelter (1982) states that because the knowledge necessary for the pursuit of goals is not uniform within society, information derived from social organizations becomes increasingly important.

There are obvious and not-so-obvious ways in which schools filled with white and wealthy students provide greater access to information about colleges and careers than schools serving mostly low-income minority students. For instance, our research on African American students from inner city St. Louis who attend predominantly white and middle-class high schools in the suburbs (Wells, Crain, & Uchetelle, in press) demonstrates that these students benefit from access to informants and well-connected acquaintances that they would not have in all-black urban schools, where less than 20% of the students go on to college. In their suburban schools they attend college fairs, are constantly reminded by their counselors and peers about college opportunities and deadlines, have access to a wealth of information on the college application process and are assigned to college counselors with strong ties to college admissions offices across the country.

Given these obvious links between network analysis and school desegregation, perpetuation theory must encompass not only Braddock's micro-level acknowledgment of racial fear and distrust on the part of isolated minorities, but also the micro-macro connections inherent in the flow of information and opportunities through interpersonal networks. The social science research presented here strongly suggests that interracial exposure in school can indeed reduce African Americans' tendency to avoid whites, and penetrate barriers between African American students and networks of information and sponsorship.

We would like to stress that we are not writing an article on the short-term effects of school desegregation — whether academic achievement or the self-esteem and self-concept of desegregated African American students. Although there are obvious overlaps with Braddock's more social-psychological view of African American fear and distrust of interracial settings and self-esteem issues, the literature on school desegregation and African American students' self-esteem is as vast as it is inconclusive (Epps, 1975; Rosenberg, 1986). While we recognize the importance of this literature for guiding school desegregation policy, we also believe, as we stated above, that the focus of school desegregation research has for too long been on these short-term effect variables, which may or may not have long-term consequences. In fact, a short-term negative impact on self-esteem may be more than compensated for in the long run if desegregated African American students gain access to higher status jobs in their adult lives. Thus, we turn to little-known research on the long-term effects of school desegregation.

Methodological Considerations

While the 21 studies discussed here provide the most significant evidence to date of the long-term effects of school desegregation on African Americans, the literature is not without shortcomings. All but four of the studies examined here are based on national longitudinal data sets, which provide a valuable cross-regional viewpoint, but do not allow for differentiation between various types of school desegregation policy — that is, the mandatory assignment plans often found in the South versus the voluntary transfer plans that are more common in the North and Midwest — and the different backgrounds, characteristics, self-concepts, and social attitudes of African American students who participate in each. These attitudinal factors, which are difficult to control in a statistical analysis, could conceivably create a spurious correlation with the main independent variable — racial makeup of school — especially for Northern African Americans, who are more likely to have personally chosen to be in desegregated schools.

In addition, studies employing national data sets cannot measure the degree of socioeconomic class desegregation that African American students experience — that is, whether they participate in an urban intradistrict desegregation plan in which they attend school with mostly low-income white students, or an interdistrict desegregation plan which allows them to attend wealthier suburban schools. In terms of perpetuation theory and its relevance to the long-term effects of school desegregation on African Americans, information on the socioeconomic status (SES) of the white students in the desegregated schools would be helpful.

Furthermore, because this article reviews a wide range of studies examining the long-term effects of school desegregation on the life chances of African Americans,[1] definitions of *segregation and desegregation* vary somewhat from study to study. Most of the researchers we cite figure school desegregation at the individual student level and not at the school district level, which means that the percentage of white students in the school attended by the respondent is considered one of many independent variables used to predict whatever dependent variable is being measured — for example, likelihood of attending a predominantly white university.

---

[1] The literature on the effects of desegregation on Hispanic Americans is much smaller and does not include studies on the long-term effects.

Unless the researchers specify a particular percentage of white students that they consider to constitute desegregation, they are comparing predominantly white "desegregated" schools to predominantly nonwhite "segregated" schools. At first blush this appears to be quite problematic; for example, a 51% white school is considered desegregated while a 51% African American school is labeled segregated. But, in reality, schools with higher non-white than white populations are generally more segregated than racially mixed schools in which whites are the majority. This is due to two factors: first, most school boards are reluctant to reassign white students to predominantly nonwhite schools and second, white parents whose children are assigned to predominantly nonwhite public schools are much more likely to place their children in private schools (Rossell & Hawley, 1981).

Because this body of research focuses on the impact of attending a predominantly white school on the life chances of African American students, it does not make much sense for these studies to employ district-level measures of desegregation, including the more sophisticated dissimilarity index used to measure district compliance with court orders and degree of white flight. These are not good measures of the institution-level effects of desegregation on the life chances of African American adults. Thus, when more complete information on the racial balance of segregated and desegregated schools in these studies is available, we provide it. Otherwise, the reader is to assume that "desegregated" schools are those that are predominantly white.

Despite these shortcomings, the long-term effects research presents some meaningful findings. Also, because the studies focus on different stages in the lives of African Americans, the work as a whole provides substantial evidence that desegregated schooling can help African Americans end perpetual segregation at different points in the life cycle. In order to trace the theory of perpetual segregation chronologically through the lives of African American students, we have divided the research into three main categories dealing with the long-term effects of school desegregation on: (a) the occupational aspirations of high school students, (b) choice of an desegregated college and subsequent educational attainment, and (c) occupational attainment and adult social networks.

Occupational Aspirations and Expectations

McPartland and Braddock (1981) point out that the black-white split in career tracks — more "socially" oriented and public-sector careers for African Americans, and more enterprising, investigative private-sector careers for whites — is not only the result of African Americans' limited access to private-sector jobs, but also the result of individual decisions that are shaped by students' secondary school experiences and the decisions of people with whom they have strong ties — their friends and family members. McPartland and Braddock (1981) note that, in high school, students' goals and decisions are strongly influenced by their peers. Similarly, Gottfredson's (1978) study of occupational development demonstrates that African American and white students hold similar occupational expectations and values when they are in elementary school, but that these interests begin to diverge toward traditional race and sex stereotypes by the end of high school.

The four studies discussed in this section attempt to measure the impact of school desegregation on African American students' occupational aspirations, but they do not represent all of the literature on school desegregation and student aspirations. For an earlier review of this literature see St. John (1975), which includes a table of 25 studies, 13 of which examine occupational aspirations, expectations or choices. Of these 13 studies, only three report a positive effect of desegregation on African American students' occupational aspirations and desegregation, while five studies show a negative effect.

We did not include the studies cited in St. John (1975) in this review because, as Hoelter (1982) notes, these early studies fail to include status attainment variables which have been shown to affect aspirations. According to Hoelter, when researchers examine aspirations they also need to understand whether respondents have developed a realistic plan of action and a clear understanding of the means one employs to attain an occupational goal. These variables play a prominent role in the application of perpetuation theory to the long-term effects of school desegregation because the networks formed through weak ties in desegregated schools are the conduits of information regarding plans of action.

Thus, the four studies reviewed here discuss the relationship between desegregated African Americans' occupational aspirations and several variables, including educational aspirations and educational achievement, designed to measure whether or not respondents are moving toward their desired career goals, and how "realistic" their plans of action are. Labeling students' occupational aspirations as "realistic" or "rational" based on prior educational achievement is controversial, especially when high aspirations on the part of low-achieving students are considered "unrealistic" or "irrational." Such labels often become self-fulfilling prophecies — part of the "cooling off" process that African American and Hispanic American students often go through as their aspirations deteriorate in the face of unequal access to high status jobs. In fact, Mickelson (1990) has argued that the students with more "concrete" attitudes toward educational and occupational chances are those who understand "the realities that people experience with respect to returns on education from the opportunity structure" (p. 45). In other words, according to Mickelson, only those African American or Hispanic American students with low occupational aspirations are being "realistic."

While we acknowledge the harsh reality of an unfair opportunity structure and the automatic disadvantages of nonwhite and low-income students, we also realize that most African American adults in high-status occupations attained those occupations through regular channels — postsecondary education and personal contacts. While nonwhite students face many more obstacles on their way to attaining an occupational goal, those students who have a clear understanding of these obstacles as well as the prerequisites for a given profession will be better prepared to achieve their goals.

In the first study, Dawkins (1983) employs a multivariate regression analysis to assess the effect of school desegregation on the occupational expectations of 3,119 African American high school seniors from 1,200 randomly selected high schools in the National Longitudinal Survey of the 1972 senior classes (NLS72). The main dependent variable, occupational expectations, was measured by the survey question, "What kind of work will you be doing when you are 30 years old?" Independent variables included school desegregation (as measured by percentage of white classmates in grades 1, 6, 9, and 12), social class, community size, high school curriculum, self-concept of ability to compete and educational aspirations. Zero-order correlations show that both male and female African American students who attend desegregated schools are more likely to expect that they will enter a professional occupation such as accounting, medicine, law or engineering — occupations that African Americans are traditionally much less likely to enter than whites.

A regression analysis shows that, relative to other factors, school desegregation continues to have a significantly positive influence on nontraditional occupational expectations for African American males who attend Southern schools ($F = 3.526$). The pattern, however, does not hold for Southern or non-Southern females ($F = .17$ and $F = .31$, respectively) or non-Southern males ($F = .018$).

Dawkins (1983) concludes that segregated schools may be part of a developmental process that channels or perpetuates African American students' expectations toward a "narrow range of traditional occupations that are low in prestige and compensation." He states that school desegregation experiences play an important part in expectations, and that individuals with no desegregation experiences in elementary and secondary schools tend to be less likely to anticipate professional careers. But he adds that for African American men from the North and African American women in general, other socialization factors such as "social class, academic aptitude and educational aspirations, high school curriculum, and self-concept of ability to complete college" also have a strong effect on the complex development of aspirations (p.110).

Hoelter (1982) attempts to analyze differences in the strategies for attaining occupational goals used by segregated and desegregated African American high school students. Citing the perpetuation of status inequality among African Americans in segregated institutions, Hoelter states that the knowledge students need concerning the association between educational and occupational attainment is usually transmitted through the interaction of students, school personnel and certain persons outside the schools system, especially parents, and is more prevalent within environments linked to the dominant white community — that is, the predominantly white school. He predicts, therefore, that school desegregation will help break the cycle of segregation by alleviating one of the mechanisms that perpetuates racial isolation: African Americans' lack of information concerning educational and occupational opportunities and methods of attaining specific goals.

Hoelter's study is based on questionnaire data from 382 male high school seniors in Louisville, KY—174 African American students attending "segregated" schools with white populations of less than 5%, and 208 students, half of whom were African American, who attended "desegregated" schools with white populations of at least 60%.[2] Using the racial composition of the high school as an independent variable, Hoelter examines what he calls the "rationality" of students' aspirations—that is, the correlation between educational plans and occupational aspirations.

> Where knowledge exists concerning the association between education and occupational attainment, and for a reasonable assessment of one's relationship to this association given self-perceptions, ability levels and ascriptions, a relatively strong affinity should exist between aspirational dimensions and these variables. (Hoelter, 1982, p. 32)

Control variables in Hoelter's study include father's occupations, father's education, family income, academic ability, grade point average, parental, and peer influence on educational plans, and students' perception of teacher's evaluation of their academic ability.[3]

Although Hoelter finds no difference between the educational aspirations of desegregated and segregated black students, and lower occupational aspirations for desegregated African Americans, he did find a higher correlation between educational and occupational aspirations — a more rational career plan — for desegregated African Americans. The zero-order correlation for whites is .639, for desegregated African Americans .470, and for segregated African Americans .361. These findings, however, are not statistically significant. But Hoelter makes another interesting find: among whites, all of the control variables positively affect educational aspirations with a multiple r of .456. The multiple r is lower for desegregated African Americans (.334) and lowest for

---

[2] All of the desegregated students were participating in a mandatory busing plan.

[3] There were no significant differences between segregated and desegregated black students on the status-origin variables.

segregated African Americans (.159). Similarly, the multiple *r* for the equation predicting the effect of control variables on occupational aspirations is .317 for whites and .351 for desegregated African Americans, but only .135 for segregated African Americans.

Hoelter concludes that black-white status inequality is perpetuated when African Americans remain segregated from the knowledge necessary for rational plans of action pertaining to status outcomes. This study also suggests that the impact of factors that help students in planning educational and occupational goals — for example, a more educated father or parental involvement in educational planning — multiplies when African American students are tied into important informational networks.

A third study of aspirations (Gable, Thompson, & Iwanicki, 1983) found significantly higher levels of career aspirations and significantly more consistent, or "rational," career planning and progression among desegregated African American students who participated in Project Concern, an interdistrict busing plan in Hartford, Connecticut. Project Concern began in 1966 and was designed as an experiment involving 265 African American students who were bused to 35 predominantly white schools in five suburban communities. Participants were randomly selected from two Hartford elementary schools in low-income areas.

Gable et al.'s (1983) sample consisted of three groups of African American students who graduated from high schools in the Hartford metropolitan area during the years of 1977–79: 45 graduates of Project Concern suburban schools, 45 Project Concern dropouts who graduated from all-African American Hartford Public Schools and 30 Hartford school graduates who were nonparticipants in the program. The study was conducted in the spring of 1980, when questionnaires pertaining to career aspirations, consistency of career planning, and career patterns were sent to prospective respondents. The researchers asked students, "When you were in high school, what type of job or career did you want to have after high school?" They found that 64% of the Project Concern graduates, 54% of the program drop-outs, and only 32% of the nonparticipants said they aspired to occupations in the upper six ranks of the North-Hatt Occupational Rating Scale. The difference between the Project Concern graduates and the nonparticipants was statistically significant ($p < .05$).

Responses to the question "What type of job or career would you like to have five years from now?" showed virtually no variation among the three groups, with 62% of the Project Concern graduates, 62% of the program dropouts, and 63% of the nonparticipants stating they wanted to have jobs/careers in the upper six ranks of the rating scale. But perhaps the most important finding of the Gable et al. study is that the career choices of the nonparticipants tended to be much less realistic and much less consistent with the actions they had taken to reach these goals. For instance, 37% of the nonparticipants, as opposed to 67% of the program graduates and 80% of the program dropouts, had career patterns — work history, postsecondary education, etc. — consistent with their occupational choices.

The Gable et al. study is particularly convincing because the African American students who were desegregated in Hartford were randomly selected. Meanwhile, the comparisons drawn between the program participants and the program dropouts allow the researchers to analyze the self-selection bias that resulted when some students chose to return to segregated urban schools. The evidence suggests that the impact of desegregation on the consistency of the career patterns of the program graduates was not artificially exaggerated, because the program dropouts also have much more consistent career patterns than the nonparticipants. This suggests that even a short-term break in the cycle of perpetual segregation can influence African American students' career goals by allowing them access to information regarding the necessary steps to achieve an occupational goal.

In another study of the aspirations and expectations of segregated and desegregated African American students, Falk (1978) surveyed a group of 184 African American sophomores in 13 segregated high schools in rural Texas counties in 1966. Two years later, when the students were seniors and half of them were enrolled in newly desegregated (predominantly white) schools, he surveyed them again with a response rate of 92%. A final survey was conducted in 1972, four years after the students had graduated from high school, and the response rate was 77% of the original sample and 84% of the first follow-up sample.

Falk found that the African American students who attended the formerly all-white schools did not, as he had hypothesized, have lower educational and occupational expectations and aspirations. In fact, by the final follow-up interviews, the desegregated students had almost significantly higher occupational aspirations ($F = 3.54$) than the segregated students. More importantly, however, Falk found that the aspirations of the desegregated students seemed more realistic since their aspired levels of education as seniors were highly correlated with their actual educational attainment four years later.

The consistency between Falk's results and those of Gable et al. seems important, despite the differences in region, type of plan (voluntary versus mandatory) and duration of plan (Gable et al.'s students were desegregated in elementary schools; Falk's for only one year). These results are also consistent with findings from a study by Wilson (1979), which will be discussed more completely in the next section. Wilson found that African American students in segregated schools who had low test scores and had been held back in school for one or more years maintained high educational aspirations, whereas desegregated African American students who had experienced similar setbacks had lowered their aspirations.

Two main conclusions can be drawn from the work reviewed in this first section on aspirations: (a) desegregated African American students set their occupational aspirations higher than do segregated African Americans and (b) desegregated African American students' occupational aspirations are more realistically related to their educational aspirations and attainment than those of segregated African American students.

The first finding, however, is not as strongly supported because only three of the four studies found this, while the fourth study, Hoelter (1982), found the opposite. Also, Dawkins (1983) found significantly higher occupational aspirations for only one of four gender-region groups. Still, these studies challenge what Kaufman and Rosenbaum (1992) refer to as the "Relative Disadvantage Hypothesis" (p. 230) — that higher standards and a greater degree of academic competition within desegregated schools will place African American students at a disadvantage and possibly lessen their self-confidence and lower their aspirations.

The second finding, concerning the rationality of aspirations, is more clearly supported, with all three of the studies that raise the issue concurring and Wilson's (1979) study offering additional support. Each of these studies bolsters Granovetter's theory of the impact of weak ties on the diffusion of influence, information, and mobility opportunities to different segments of society, since the most important aspect of realistic expectations is an understanding of the requirements for particular occupations. The following section provides greater evidence of he more micro-level aspects of perpetuation theory.

Choice of College and Educational Attainment

This second section of the literature on the long-term effects of school desegregation tests a critical element of perpetuation theory: the link between the racial balance of African American students' high schools and their participation in higher education. The first four of the nine studies discussed in this section are mainly concerned with whether African American students attend desegregated colleges. (One also examines which academic majors African American college students select.) The remaining five studies focus on college survival and educational attainment.

This review of literature does not address the pros and cons for African American students of attending predominantly white and historically African American colleges. While we are aware of arguments in favor of African American universities, we realize that to delve into that debate would constitute a second article. We do, however, assume that there are some social benefits to attending predominantly white universities, at least for some African American students. Our reasons for this assumption are based in perpetuation theory and its discussion of the flow of information and influence through institutions. If nothing else, we would argue that African American students should not be prohibited from attending predominantly white universities by fear of whites and desegregated settings.

In the article in which he first develops perpetuation theory, Braddock (1980) analyzes survey data from 253 randomly selected African American students enrolled in two predominantly African American and two predominantly white colleges in Florida. He constructs a model of "determinants of attendance" at desegregated versus segregated colleges using structural equations and multiple regression analysis. The model contains five causal steps: (a) socioeconomic level and sex, (b) high school racial composition, (c) high school grades, (d) financial aid, college cost and college reputation, and (e) racial composition of the college attended.

Braddock finds that high school racial composition exhibits one of the largest (.23) direct effects on attendance at a predominantly white college. Only high school grades (.23) and college costs (-.27) show larger effects. In fact, the effect of high school racial composition on attendance at a predominantly white college is mediated only slightly (.01) by grade point average. This is true, notes Braddock, even though the percentage of whites in the high school is significantly inversely related (-.13) to class rank.

> This finding bolsters the argument that desegregation practice affords black students the opportunity to develop confidence in their scholastic abilities and their adaptive and coping skills in majority white settings even though their scholastic performances are likely to gain them less recognition than they could expect to receive in predominantly or all-black educational settings. (Braddock, 1980, p. 184)

Furthermore, the percentage of white students in a desegregated high school appears to have an effect on the African American student's choice of a predominantly white college. African Americans who attended high schools that were at least 75% white attended predominantly white colleges at more than twice the rate (70% versus 33%) of African Americans who went to high schools that were less than 25% white.

The second study that looks at African American students' college attendance (Braddock & McPartland, 1982) employs the NLS72 database with survey responses from more than 3,000 African American students. Using a regression analysis and controlling for the sex, SES, and academic qualifications of the students, Braddock and McPartland find that the racial composition of African American students' high schools had an effect on postsecondary educational attainment, with students who attended desegregated schools showing higher attainment. The effect is small in the South (Beta = .02), and although it approaches statistical significance in the North (Beta = .09), social class background and academic achievement test scores are the strongest determinants of years of college attainment.

When they examine attainment at predominantly white colleges only, Braddock and McPartland find that the net effect of elementary and secondary school desegregation is positive and significant for both Southern (Beta = .15) and Northern (Beta = .11) African American students. Moreover, in the South, early school desegregation appears to be roughly equal in importance as a determinant of years of attainment in a predominantly white

college to SES and academic qualification. In the North, achievement test scores are shown as the major determinant of years of
attainment in a predominantly white college, followed by high
school grades, racial composition of high school and SES.[4] Some
of this increase in college attendance for desegregated African
Americans in the North, however, is due to higher enrollment at
white two-year colleges.

Another study (Braddock, 1987) of the higher education
experiences of desegregated African American students uses the
more recent longitudinal data from the High School and Beyond
survey, a national sample of sophomores and seniors, including
3,119 African Americans. The original sample was collected in
1980, with follow-ups conducted in 1982 and 1984.

A multiple regression analysis reveals that in both the North
and the South, the racial composition of a African American
student's high school exhibits a much larger effect on the racial
makeup of the college he/she will likely attend than any of the
other factors measured — sex, SES, high school test scores, high
school grades, and proximity of the college to home. Yet these
findings also show that the African American graduates of desegregated high schools who go on to institutions of higher
education are slightly less likely to attend four-year colleges than
their counterparts from predominantly African American high
schools (58% versus 61%). Braddock (1987) attributes the "unexpected pattern" of higher two-year college attendance among
African American graduates of predominantly white schools
largely to the strong tendency for such students to choose white
institutions over African American ones, "even to the extent of
enrolling at a two-year white college instead of a four-year African
American college" (p. 10).

Braddock also measures the degree to which attending a
predominantly white high school affects African American
students' choices of nontraditional college majors such as the
sciences and technology. The findings demonstrate that African
American graduates of predominantly white high schools are five
times as likely to major in architecture, and nearly four times as
likely to major in computer and information sciences, as African

---

[4] The effect is probably somewhat weaker in the North because there are few
predominantly black four-year colleges in that area.

American graduates of segregated schools. Results are smaller and more mixed for fields such as mathematics, engineering, physical sciences, and pre-med and pre-dental programs. Among nontechnical fields, graduates of segregated schools were more likely to major in art, music, psychology, and the social sciences than were their desegregated counterparts. In vocational fields, male graduates of desegregated schools were twice as likely to major in computer programming, and five times as likely to major in electronics, as segregated high school graduates. These students were also less likely to enroll in traditional African American male programs such as auto mechanics and welding. Female desegregated students were less frequently found in secretarial and clerical training programs, and home economics.

A multiple regression analysis, which includes the independent variables of sex, SES, high school tests, high school grades, high school region, high school racial composition, and college racial composition, shows that in two-year colleges, high school racial composition is second only to high school test scores as a determinant of African American students majoring in technical and scientific subfields. In four-year colleges, racial composition is third behind sex and high school test scores in steering African American students toward these majors.

The final study to focus on the link between desegregated schools and desegregated colleges, Dawkins (1991), is discussed in more depth in the following section. Dawkins analyzes a previously unused data set, the National Survey of Black Americans, which includes several questions on racial issues that are missing from other national surveys. Dawkins conducts eight separate analyses using three different measures of postsecondary school interracial contact and finds that high school racial composition is generally a good predictor of interracial contact for African American adults, with African American students who attend predominantly white schools most likely to interact with whites as adults. The strongest variable in Dawkins' analysis is the effect of high school racial composition on the racial composition of the college attended.

Crain and Mahard (1978) examine a random sample of 2,150 African American high school seniors from NLS72 to estimate African American students' college attendance and survival rates (percent matriculated to junior year) based on the percentage of white students in their classes at various grade levels. Controlling for mean SES and school district size, Crain and Mahard found that African American graduates of all-African American schools in the South had college attendance rates 5% higher, and college survival rates that were 6% higher, than their counterparts in desegregated schools. But in the North, the opposite was true: college attendance rates were 8% higher for African American graduates of desegregated schools, and college survival rates were 10% higher for African Americans from predominantly white schools.

The most obvious of the possible explanations for the North-South differences is that the segregated Southern African Americans were tied into a network of African American colleges that do not exist in the North. Secondly, few desegregated Southern African Americans had been desegregated for more than a few years in 1972, a weak desegregation treatment. But the most worrisome aspect of the Crain and Mahard conclusion is the possibility of self-selection among the Northern African Americans. Because there was little court-ordered desegregation in the North in 1972, African American students from this region who attended desegregated schools were likely to come from families that purposely sought desegregated neighborhoods and schools.

Crain and Mahard (1978) attempt to address the issue of self-selection by reanalyzing their data according to racial desegregation by school district rather than by school. They state that if the relationship between racial composition and student outcomes is due to self-selection, they should find that low-segregation districts do not differ from high segregation districts in African American student outcomes. Yet what they find is that for college attendance there is a smaller gap between whites and African Americans in low-segregation districts, suggesting that desegregation had a genuine effect.

Still, in a comment on Crain and Mahard, Eckland (1978) points out that "it is not the percentage of whites in a school that necessarily affects African American performance, but *who* these whites are" (p. 123). He states that one cannot assume that a district-level analysis will adequately control for self-selection, since it is not only African Americans but also, and perhaps to a greater degree, whites who self-select.

Self-selection is also an issue in an earlier study by Crain (1971). Employing a survey of 1,600 African American adults living in Northern metropolitan areas, Crain found that those who had attended desegregated schools (at least half-white and not undergoing rapid racial transition) were more likely to have graduated from high school and attended college; they also scored higher on verbal tests than those who had attended segregated schools. Nearly half (48%) of the respondents from segregated schools did not finish high school, while only 36% of the respondents from desegregated schools did not graduate. Similarly, only 24% of Northern-born men from segregated schools went on to college, while 32% of Northern-born men from desegregated schools did so. Among men who had migrated from the South to the North by age 10, the difference in college attendance for graduates of desegregated versus segregated schools is even greater: 30% versus 3%. (Differences for women are similar but smaller.) Respondents who had attended segregated elementary schools and desegregated high schools (or vice-versa) seemed more like the desegregated group than the segregated one.

After controlling for a number of variables, Crain found that only a small portion of the difference between segregated and desegregated African Americans was due to family background. For instance, among the Northern-born respondents, 42% of those who had attended desegregated schools had mothers who had completed high school, compared to 38% of alumni of segregated schools. These findings, Crain contends, somewhat dispel concerns about the impact of self-selection. He concludes that the higher educational attainment and academic achievement of African Americans who attend desegregated schools is only partly the result of a higher quality of education; it is also, he states, the result of the "decisive impact" of desegregation on African Americans' first-hand knowledge of the requirement to succeed in a predominantly white society (p. 25).

In a similar, but nationwide, study of 1,400 African American adults who had originally been surveyed as college freshmen in 1971, Green (1982) conducted a 1979–80 follow-up survey which asked the African American adults about their educational attainment, occupations and income. The follow-up also asked respondents about the racial composition of their high schools and the neighborhoods where they had grown up. A simple regression employed to identify factors predicting undergraduate academic performance found the three most influential variables to be high school grades ($r = .34$), sex (female $r = .21$) and attendance of a predominantly minority high school ($r = -.11$). Green concludes that although African Americans who attended minority high schools had better high school grades, they usually ended up with lower college grades and felt they were less prepared for college than their peers from desegregated schools. "One consistent finding is the negative impact of minority secondary schools on the academic performance of African American college students" (p. 65). Green suggests that such findings possibly result from minority high schools' tendency to inflate grades. Still, attending a minority high school did not appear to influence other educational outcomes such as persistence in higher education and entry to graduate school. Another possibility has less to do with academic preparation per se, but rather with the pressures students face as they move from high school to college — pressures that could intensify if students move from racially segregated to racially desegregated institutions.

The Wilson (1979) study, which was mentioned briefly in the previous section, employs longitudinal data from a nationally representative sample[5] of 2,213 male students from 87 public high schools. African American students account for 256, or about 12%, of the total sample. The first interviews were conducted in 1966 when the students were in 10th grade; the final of four follow-up interviews was conducted in the summer of 1970, one year after the students graduated from high school. The sample attrition rate, about equal for African Americans and whites, was approximately 27%.

Wilson's analysis of the data was designed to assess how the educational attainment process differs among African Americans of different social classes and African Americans of segregated versus desegregated schools. Using an educational attainment model, similar in design to a status attainment model, Wilson developed five causal steps of analysis: (a) SES level and mental ability, (b) academic performance and pacing (advancement from one grade to the next), (c) self-concept of ability, self-esteem and disciplinary problems in school, (d) educational aspirations, and (e) educational attainment. He examines the interaction effects between segregated/desegregated school context and high/low SES on the causal variables in each stage of the model.

---

[5]   Bachman's "Youth in Transition" survey.

Wilson finds that desegregation exerted little *direct* influence on the African American attainment processes, although it was positively related to mental ability, self-concept of ability, and educational attainment, and negatively related to self-esteem. Yet, when he employs a regression analysis to test for the interaction effects of desegregation on the five-step educational attainment model, he discovers that educational attainment can be much more easily predicted for African Americans from desegregated schools: the R^2 for an equation using school performance variables, attitudinal variables and SES is .58 for alumni of desegregated schools, but only .31 for those from segregated schools. Pacing, disciplinary problems and SES are the three variables that carry more weight in the desegregated setting. Therefore, African Americans in desegregated schools who are held back a grade are more likely to drop out than those held back in segregated schools, while African Americans who skip a grade in desegregated schools are more likely to go on to college than those who skip a grade in segregated schools. Meanwhile, desegregation increases the negative impact of disciplinary problems on educational attainment and the coefficient of socioeconomic level on educational attainment is twice as large in the desegregated as in the segregated subsample. According to Wilson, the finding on SES suggests that parental achievement is more easily converted into advantages for offspring when the children attend desegregated schools. Wilson's findings suggest, therefore, that school desegregation, in and of itself, will not affect class bias in aspirations, which affect whites as well as African Americans.

Although the differences between the desegregated and segregated African American subsamples were independent of those created by the divergence between upper- and lower-class African Americans, the differences mirrored each other, with the upper-class status being more powerfully affected by disciplinary problems and pacing. The class interaction effects, however, were generally weaker than the desegregation interaction effects.

The Wilson study has two important shortcomings. First, the subsamples of African American students are so small as to create suspicion that some of the results are due to sampling deficiencies. Second, Wilson relied on the self-reporting of students for academic achievement.

In a more recent study, Kaufman and Rosenbaum (1992) found that African American students from inner city Chicago who moved to predominantly white suburbs through the Gautreaux housing desegregation program were more likely to finish high school and go on to college than Gautreaux participants who had been relocated within the city. Reasons cited included suburban teachers and counselors who helped prepare their children for postsecondary education and were "in touch" with colleges. Parents and students spoke of the advantages of attending a high school where there was a constant flow of information about scholarships and college visits and where classmates' older brothers and sisters had gone to college and could offer help and advice to their younger siblings.

In this study, the overall rate of college attendance was significantly higher for suburban-movers than city-movers. Also, of those students who did go on to college, the suburban-movers were more likely to attend four-year (versus two year) institutions and to work towards bachelor's (versus associate's) degrees. Obviously, there are self-selection issues inherent in this study, even though Gautreaux participants were randomly selected from the pool of applicants. Still, the choice to move to suburban rather than urban housing under this program signals a predisposition to desegregated settings on the part of the suburban-movers.

The major conclusion to be drawn from the studies examined in this section is that African American graduates of desegregated schools are more likely than those of segregated schools to attend desegregated colleges. This section, therefore, provides support for Braddock's (1980) micro-view of perpetuation, which depicts the tendency of African Americans to perpetuate racial segregation — in this case, by choosing a predominantly African American college over a predominantly white one — when they have not experienced desegregated situations.

As for the educational attainment of desegregated African Americans, the research (with the obvious exception of Crain and Mahard's findings on Southern students) generally supports the conclusion that African Americans from desegregated schools will have greater educational attainment. Still, the findings of Braddock and McPartland (1982) and Braddock (1987) concerning the greater tendency of desegregated African Americans to head toward two-year rather than four-year colleges, especially in the North, are disturbing, but partly mitigated by the Kaufman and Rosenbaum findings. Issues of classmates' social class and the quality of education available at two-year colleges in this country, which are not addressed in this literature make these findings and the classless basis of perpetuation theory more tenuous. At the same time, Braddock's (1987) findings on college majors are promising and underscore the need for more research on the different educational experiences of African Americans in two- and four-year colleges.

Occupational Attainment and Adult Social Networks

The conclusions from the previous section, while focusing more on individual choices and micro issues, also lend additional support to the more macro-level aspects of perpetuation theory: that African American students who attend desegregated colleges are more likely to gain social contacts (not to mention a credential from an institution of higher social status) that will help them attain higher occupational status and income later in life. The questions raised in this final section will further test this aspect of our theory.

The earliest research on this topic was conducted by Crain (1970) when he examined data from a 1966 survey of 1,231 African Americans, ages 21 to 45, who lived in Northern metropolitan areas, had attended Northern high schools, and reported having an occupation. Using the 1960 Census, Crain established a list of "traditional" African American occupations—mostly lower blue-collar jobs, such as service work and labor, and lower white-collar jobs, such as clerical work.

In a basic analysis of the relationship between current occupation and having attended a segregated or desegregated high school, Crain found that one-third of the respondents who had attended desegregated high schools were in three nontraditional African American occupations: crafts, sales, and the professions. Only one-fifth of the respondents who had attended segregated schools were employed in these fields. African American women from desegregated schools were also more likely to enter the professions, though equally likely to hold traditional jobs.

Crain also found that African Americans who had attended desegregated high schools had higher occupational prestige and higher incomes: In 1968, the annual income of African American alumni of desegregated schools was about $1,000 higher than that of segregated school graduates. After controlling for background variables such as age, stability of family of origin, and educational attainment, Crain estimated that about two-thirds of the difference in income between desegregated and segregated adults was due to differences in educational attainment. The rest appeared to be attributable to differences in social networks. For example, among those respondents who did not attend college, the alumni of desegregated schools had a much higher percentage of friends who had graduated from college (62% versus 44% for male respondents; 47% versus 33% for females). Still, given that the respondents in this study attended high school during the 1950s and early 1960s in the North, the chances that these African Americans were involuntarily bused to a desegregated school are slim, which means that the same self-selection bias found in other studies is inherent in these results.

A more recent study by Crain and Strauss (1985) on the same subject is less contaminated by self-selection bias. Like the Gable et al. study discussed in the first section, the Crain and Strauss paper is based on Project Concern, the experimentally designed school desegregation program in Hartford. Two portions of the original 1966 Project Concern sample were randomly selected and a control group was created. Additional randomly selected groups of students were desegregated between 1968 and 1971, but control groups were not created for each of these cohorts. Students in all three cohorts graduated in 1983, unless, of course, they had dropped out of school.

The findings of the first stage of the Crain and Strauss study, which compares the graduates of Project Concern to the graduates of the Hartford public schools, reveal that by 1985, participation in Project Concern appears to have had no effect on unemployment rates but a significant positive effect on full-time college enrollment. Of those students who did not go on to college, the Project Concern students were more likely to be in nontraditional African American occupations, including the four "whitest" occupations according to the Census Bureau: sales, entertainment, private sector professional and managerial positions, and high-level private-sector white-collar positions. These jobs were held by only 8% of the male control group but 23% of the male Project Concern participants. Among females, 34% of Project Concern graduates, but only 20% of the control group, held such positions.

Also, female Project Concern participants (but not males) were much more likely to be working with mostly white co-workers than females in the control group (72% versus 58%), and both male and female participants described their chances of promotion as good at a significantly higher rate than members of the control group (65% versus 48% for males and 49% versus 39% for females).

Despite the unique experimental design of the Project Concern program, these findings are somewhat biased by self-selection because they exclude those students who dropped out of the program. Therefore, in the next step of the analysis, Crain and Strauss add to the "experiment" group data those students who were randomly selected to participate in Project Concern, but who either never attended a suburban school or who attended and then dropped out of the program and returned to the Hartford schools. In addition, students who had dropped out of the Hartford schools or left to attend private schools were figured in as part of the control group.

With this larger sample, Crain and Strauss control for factors such as educational attainment, family background and age, and find that, for males, the effect of participating in Project Concern on the likelihood of being employed in a private white-collar or service occupation is weaker than either family background or educational attainment. For females, however, the opposite is true: Project Concern participation is the strongest predictor in two of the three equations, and stronger than family background in the third.

Crain and Strauss conclude that when self-selection bias is removed, it appears as though school desegregation does not have much effect on the occupational attainment of African American men with no college education, except indirectly through educational attainment. Still, it is important to note that college students are missing from this sample, and that the participants of Project Concern were much more likely to go to college than those in the control group. Furthermore, the findings concerning African American women who attended suburban schools through Project Concern are impressive. Given that these students did not attend college but went straight into the labor market, weak ties established in a suburban school could have influenced their job placement.

Just how school desegregation can contribute to African American students' success in the labor market is the topic of study by Braddock and McPartland (1987). Using a national survey of 4,078 employers, the researchers describe the actual practices used in recruiting prospective employees.

The data show that the employers' most popular methods of recruiting job candidates for lower- or entry-level positions are (a) unsolicited "walk-in" applications, (b) informal referrals from current employees (e.g., via social networks), and (c) referrals from public employment agencies. Informal referrals and unsolicited walk-in applications are also among the most frequent methods used by employers in creating college-educated candidate pools. Other recruitment methods, such as placing ads in newspapers, are used less frequently, especially in recruiting for higher level jobs. Therefore, the authors argue that minorities who experience "social network segregation" find limited opportunities as job candidates. In fact, the chances are significantly greater than an opening for a job requiring a college degree will be filled by whites when informal referrals via social networks are used as a major employer recruitment method. For middle-level and lower-level jobs, there is no sizable or consistent employment benefit to whites or minorities that depends upon whether the employer recruits through social networks. "This is explained because white social networks may be tied to higher quality jobs" (Braddock & McPartland, 1987, p. 9).

In the second phase of this study, Braddock and McPartland combine the survey of employers with data from the NLS72 and use the racial makeup of the African American students' high schools to identify their social networks as desegregated or segregated. They find that African American high school graduates who used social networks to find jobs earn less, on average, if their networks were segregated than if they had not used networks at all. They earned more if they used desegregated networks rather than no network.

The analysis of the data, however, is based on the assumption that African American students who attended desegregated schools will have desegregated social networks. In fact, these networks would vary largely depending on the racial makeup of the schools and the degree to which students are "desegregated" within their schools. Still, Granovetter would argue that even the weakest of African American-white social networks is better than no interracial network at all. Meanwhile, as discussed in the second section, the value of desegregated social networks would be contingent on the SES of the white students.

Braddock and McPartland also find that when an employer makes a final hiring decision based on a pool of applicants, segregated minority candidates are at a special disadvantage because the employer is likely to ask about their previous employment experiences or request references from school or employment officials. White employers are less likely to be familiar with a African American school, a African American clergy, or a African American firm. Thus, simply attending a predominantly white school provides students with an important link to white employers. In addition, if they can use teachers and counselors at a white school as references, their weak ties are more likely to pay off than stronger ties to educators in all-African American schools.

In a separate study of the employers of NLS72 respondents, Braddock, Crain, McPartland, and Dawkins (1986) demonstrate that the type of high school, inner city or suburban, attended by a African American graduate does play a role in whether or not he or she will be hired by a white-owned business. On the basis of more than 1,000 responses from business owners and personnel managers at small and large white-owned companies across the nation, the researchers found that hypothetical African American male graduates of suburban high schools were assigned to jobs roughly 3⅔ points (based on a socioeconomic index) higher in occupational prestige than hypothetical African American male graduates of inner city high schools. According to the survey,

> knowledge that a job candidate graduated from a suburban school with a good reputation rather than an inner city school is likely to signal to employers that the quality of education was better in the suburban school, and for blacks it may also suggest to employers that the job candidates are likely to be more experienced in functioning in interracial situations. (Braddock et al., 1986, p.13)

Another study that looked at employer hiring and remuneration practices focused on 180 African Americans with MBA degrees (Brown & Ford, 1977). The authors found that African American MBAs from predominantly African American universities received starting salaries that were substantially lower than those of their white counterparts, while, on the average, the African American MBAs from predominantly white universities received starting salaries that were almost $10,000 higher than white MBA starting salaries. In other words, African American graduates of predominantly white MBA programs end up with the highest starting salaries of all MBAs.

In a study of 800 African American and white male college alumni who had graduated between 1931 and 1964 from two desegregated universities and one predominantly African American university, Althauser and Spivack (1975) found that the African American graduates of the predominantly African American school were much less likely to have entered business (self-employed or salaried) but more likely to have entered a profession (especially medicine) than either the African American or white graduates of the desegregated universities. The African American graduates of the segregated college were more than twice as likely to be in social work as the African American graduates of the two desegregated universities; they also tended to acquire first jobs with slightly less status than those acquired by the African American and white graduates of the desegregated institutions. Althauser and Spivack also found the gap in mean incomes ($200–$600 in 1957–59 dollars) between African American and white graduates of the desegregated universities to be smaller than the gap in mean incomes between the white college graduates and the African Americans who graduated from the predominantly African American university ($1,400–$1,600).

A more recent study on the "social-psychological processes" of minority segregation in the labor market (Braddock & McPartland, 1989) attempts to measure the perpetuation of segregation across institutions. The data for this analysis, based on the National Longitudinal Surveys Youth Cohort, includes 602 males and 472 females from five ethnic and class subgroups who were between the ages of 14 and 21 in 1979. Control variables include age, sex, employment sector, occupational level, high school racial composition, race of co-workers, co-worker friendliness, and supervisor competence.

The data indicate that, among both white-collar and blue-collar full-time workers, young African American adults who attended segregated schools are less likely to have white work associates than their counterparts from white-majority schools, although they are somewhat more likely to have white-collar jobs. A multiple regression analysis reveals that high school racial composition is the most powerful determinant of occupational segregation. And while this relationship is stronger in the North than in the South, high school racial composition is the only significant predictor of co-worker race in either region.

In a recent study that measures an important micro variable — the attitudes of graduates from segregated and desegregated schools toward other-race co-workers — Trent (1991) examines the 1979 cohort of the National Longitudinal Survey of Youth Labor and Market Experience. He uses three questions from different waves of the survey: (a) the racial composition of the respondents' high schools, (b) the racial composition of their work groups, and (c) their perception of co-workers as friendly or unfriendly.

Trent finds that African American, Hispanic American, and white graduates of segregated schools perceive racially mixed work groups as less friendly than racially homogenous ones. For African American respondents the difference is three-fourths of a standard deviation; for Hispanic Americans it is about one fourth of a standard deviation; and for whites, it is one-third of a standard deviation. Respondents from desegregated schools make much less of a distinction; one-half of a standard deviation for African Americans, one-third of a standard deviation for Hispanic Americans; and one-tenth of a standard deviation for whites. This suggests that desegregated school experiences have a long-term diminishing effect on negative feelings toward co-workers of other ethnic groups in later life.

Trent also finds that minority graduates of desegregated high schools are much more likely to work in firms with greater numbers of white employees, even when controlling for the racial composition of the country. This would imply that minority graduates of desegregated high schools also have higher occupational status and income, because firms with greater numbers of white employees tend to offer positions of higher occupational status and higher income. Trent does not find, however, that minorities from desegregated schools have higher occupational prestige or income than do those from segregated schools. This may be due to imperfections in the multiple regression analysis; Trent did not control for spurious factors such as size of the town, and desegregated schools tend to be in small towns.

In the same recent study that was mentioned in the second section, Dawkins (1991) uses the National Survey of Black Americans in eight separate analyses of postsecondary school interracial contact. As was mentioned, the strongest single variable in Dawkins's analysis is the effect of high school racial composition on the racial composition of the college attended.

When looking at the later life experiences of the respondents, Dawkins finds that, for the three age groups under 40, there is a reasonably strong positive relationship — very strong for the youngest and declining slightly for the respondents in their 30s — between desegregated school attendance and interracial contact as adults. He also finds that alumni of desegregated high schools have higher occupational attainment, controlling for socioeconomic background factors. Results are weak and inconsistent for respondents from the South, but there is a consistent positive effect among the three youngest age groups of non-Southerners. There is also a consistent positive effect of high school racial composition on the racial composition of the neighborhood the respondent lives in as an adult, but the effect is not very large.

The Green study (1982), which was also cited in the previous section, includes a segment on the social and professional networks of African Americans who attended segregated and desegregated high schools. Green found that eight years after entering college, African Americans who had attended minority high schools were less likely to be employed in racially-mixed work environments or to have established social relationships with whites. African Americans who had grown up in desegregated neighborhoods were more likely to work in racially-mixed work environments and to develop social relationships with whites. High school desegregation did not, however, predict income or occupational attainment, nor did neighborhood desegregation influence college grades, degree attainment, or income.

Three major conclusions can be drawn from the studies cited in this section: (a) desegregated African American students are more likely to have desegregated social and professional networks later in life, (b) desegregated African Americans are more likely to find themselves in desegregated employment, and (c) desegregated African Americans are more likely to be working in white-collar and professional jobs in the private sector than African Americans from segregated schools, who are more likely to be in government and blue-collar jobs, although there is less consistent evidence for this last finding.

Conclusion

Beginning with the aspirations of high school students and ending with tangible results of African American adults' social networks and participation in the work force, our analysis has attempted to trace the path of perpetual segregation and isolation, pointing out the various junctures at which the cycle can be broken by African American students who have access to information about better educational and occupational opportunities and who are less fearful of whites. We believe that this review supports the theory that interracial contact in elementary or secondary school can help African Americans overcome perpetual segregation.

There is a strong possibility, based on the last section of the literature, that when occupational attainment is dependent on knowing the right people and being in the right place at the right time, school desegregation assists African American students in gaining access to traditionally "white" jobs. It is not clear, however, based on these studies of the occupational attainment of desegregated African American students, whether the social networks of the individual students, or the biases and prejudices of the employers who favor prospective employees who "act white" and are graduates of predominantly white schools, has a greater impact on the job prospects of desegregated African Americans. It is also important to note that the self-selection bias discussed earlier in this paper becomes more difficult to measure as we consider its effects on desegregated-versus-segregated African American occupational attainment. It is quite likely, for instance, that some of the personal characteristics of African American students that would lead them to choose a desegregated school — less fear of whites, more motivation to achieve in a "white world," etc. — are similar to the characteristics sought by white employers in prospective employees. These personality traits are not easily measured by such variables as SES, sex, or age.

Obviously, more research must follow — research conducted at the local level where researchers can better assess the specific impact of various desegregation plans. Such research would help discern much of the self-selection bias reported in the studies presented here; it would also allow closer examination of the impact of socioeconomic desegregation on African American students. For instance, a study comparing long-term effects of a mandatory intradistrict busing program with those of a voluntary interdistrict plan would allow a close evaluation of the differences between African American students who self-select desegregated schools and those who are assigned to them, while also allowing researchers to compare long-term effects for African American students desegregated into high- versus low-SES schools.

Still the questions raised by this review should give a new focus to the current debate on whether or not to dismantle existing school desegregation plans. That new focus should move away from an overemphasis on test score comparisons and toward questions of long-term effects and the life chances of African American and Hispanic American students. If we return to the original purpose of school desegregation litigation — to provide African Americans with equal access to high-status educational institutions and the social networks within them — the longer-term effects could well be higher test scores and improved academic achievement for future generations of African American students.

References

Althauser, R. P., & Spivack, S. S. (1975). *The unequal elites.* New York: John Wiley & Sons.

Braddock, J. H. (1980). The perpetuation of segregation across levels of education: A behavioral assessment of the contact-hypothesis. *Sociology of Education, 53*, 178–186.

Braddock, J. H. (1987). *Segregated high school experiences and black students' college and major field choices.* Paper presented at the National Conference on School Desegregation, Chicago, IL.

Braddock, J. H., Crain, R. L., McPartland, J. M., & Dawkins, R. L. (1986). Applicant race and job placement decisions: A national survey experiment. *International Journal of Sociology and Social Policy, 6*, 3–24.

Braddock, J. H., & McPartland, J. M. (1982). Assessing school desegregation effects: New directions in research. *Research in Sociology of Education and Socialization, 3*, 259–282.

Braddock, J. H., & McPartland, J. M. (1987). How minorities continue to be excluded from equal employment opportunities: Research on labor market and institutional barriers. *Journal of Social Issues, 43*, 5–39.

Braddock, J. H., & McPartland, J. M. (1989). Social-psychological processes that perpetuate racial segregation: The relationship between school and employment desegregation. *Journal of Black Studies, 19,* 267–289.

Brown, H. A., & Ford, D. L. (1977). An exploratory analysis of discrimination in the employment of black MBA graduates. *Journal of Applied Psychology, 62*, 5–56.

Crain, R. L. (1970). School integration and occupational achieve ment of Negroes. *The American Journal of Sociology, 75*, 593–606.

Crain, R. L. (1971). School integration and the academic achievement of Negroes. *Sociology of Education, 44*, 1–26.

Crain, R. L., & Mahard, R. (1978). School racial compositions and black college attendance and achievement test performance. *Sociology of Education, 51*, 81–101.

Crain, R. L., & Strauss, J. (1985). *School desegregation and black occupational attainments: Results from a long-term experiment* (Rep. No. 359). Baltimore, MD: Center for the Social Organization of Schools.

Dawkins, M. P. (1983). Black students' occupational expecta tions: A national study of the impact of school desegregation. *Urban Education, 18*, 98–113.

Dawkins, M. P. (1991). *Long-term effects of school de-segregation on African Americans: Evidence from the national survey of black Americans.* Unpublished paper.

Eckland, B. K. (1978). School racial composition and college attendance revisited. *Sociology of Education, 53*, 122–125.

Epps, E. G. (1975). The impact of school desegregation on aspir-ations, self-concepts and other aspects of personality. *Law and Contemporary Problems, 39*, 300–313.

Falk, W. W. (1978). Mobility attitudes of segregated and de-segregated black youths. *Journal of Negro Education, 3*, 132–142.

Gable, R. K., Thompson, D. L., & Iwanicki, E. F. (1983). The effects of voluntary desegregation on occupational outcomes. *The Vocational Guidance Quarterly, 31*, 230–239.

Gottfredson, L. S. (1978). *Race and sex differences in occupa tional aspirations: Their development and consequences for occupational segregation* (Rep. No. 254). Baltimore, MD: Center for Social Organization of Schools.

Granovetter, M. (1973). The strength of weak ties. *American Journal of Sociology, 78*, 1360–1380.

Granovetter, M. (1983). The strength of weak ties: A network theory revisited. In R. Collins (Ed.), *Sociological Theory* (Vol. I) (pp. 201–233). San Francisco: Jossey-Bass.

Granovetter, M. (1986). The micro-structure of school de-segregation. In J. Prager, D. Longshore, & M. Seeman (Eds.), *School desegregation research: New directions in situational analysis* (pp. 81–110). New York: Plenum Press.

Green K. C. (1982). *Integration and educational attainment: A longitudinal study of the effects of integration on black educational attainment and occupational outcomes.* Unpublished doctoral dissertation, University of California-Los Angeles.

Hoelter, J. W. (1982). Segregation and rationality in black status aspiration process. *Sociology of Education, 55,* 31–39.

Kaufman, J. E., & Rosenbaum, J. (1992). The education and employment of low income black youth in white suburbs. *Education Evaluation and Policy Analysis, 14,* 229–240.

Kluger, R. (1975). *Simple justice.* New York: Vintage Books.

Levin, H. M. (1975). Education, life chances, and the courts: The role of social science evidence. *Law and Contemporary Problems,* 39, 217–240.

Lin, N. (1990). Social resources and instrumental action. In R. Breiger (Ed.), *Social Mobility and Social Structure* (pp. 247–271). Cambridge: Cambridge University Press.

McPartland, J. M., & Braddock, J. H. (1981). Going to college and getting a good job: The impact of desegregation. In W. D. Hawley (Ed.), *Effective School Desegregation: Equality, Quality and Feasibility* (pp. 141–154). London: Sage Publications.

Mickelson, R. A. (1990). The attitude-achievement paradox among black adolescents. *Sociology of Education, 63,* 44–61.

Montgomery, J. D. (1992). Job search and network composition: Implications for the strength-of-weak-ties hypothesis. *American Sociological Review, 57,* 586–596.

Prager, J., Longshore, D., & Seeman, M. (1986). The de-segregation situation. In J. Prager, D. Longshore, & M. Seeman (Eds.), *School Desegregation Research: New Directions in Situational Analysis* (pp. 3–18). New York: Plenum Press.

Rosenberg, M. (1986). Self-esteem research: A phenomenological corrective. In J. Prager, D. Longshore, & M. Seeman (Eds.), *School Desegregation Research: New Directions in Situational Analysis* (pp. 175–199). New York: Plenum Press.

Rossell, C., & Hawley, W. (1981). Understanding white flight and doing something about it. In W. D. Hawley (Ed.), *Effective School Desegregation: Equality, Quality and Feasibility* (pp. 157–184). London: Sage Publications.

St. John, N. (1975). *School desegregation: Outcomes for children.* New York: John Wiley & Sons.

Trent, W. (1991). *Desegregation and analysis report.* New York: The Legal Defense and Educational Fund.

Wells, A. S., Crain, R. L., & Uchetelle, S. (in press). *Stepping over the color line: Black inner-city students in suburban schools.* New Haven, CT: Yale University Press.

Wilson, K. L. (1979). The effects of integration and class on black educational attainment. *Sociology of Education, 53,* 84–98.

Wilson, W. J. (1987). *The truly disadvantaged: The inner city, the underclass, and public policy.* Chicago: University of Chicago Press.

CHAPTER 15

THERE'S NO PLACE LIKE HOME

Jim Garvin

In 1954, the Supreme Court found in the *Brown* decision that education was, in fact, set in a social context. Neither neutral by being separate nor equal by being apart, education was declared by the Court to sit in the visceral midst of society. In so doing, education was both marked and urged to become the arbiter of social change for this country. Now, some 40 years after that decision, education is still set in a social context. Yet, rather than becoming an arbiter of change, education may have become nothing more than a reflection of the use of social power and how that power determines social place. Rather than education flowing outward with its effects on society, society may instead flow inward to schools, into the lives of children, etching human drawings in the still separate colors of black and white. Nowhere is this more clearly seen than in the urban school systems of this country. Moreover, those urban schools are situated in a unique and socially constructed physical environment.

All urban space is contested ground (Andrews, 1987; Davis, 1991; Gottdiener, 1985; Katznelson, 1985). The urban space of New Orleans is no exception and the struggle for that space is a story of the use of power and the perception of power, which gives the conflict its own texture (Miron, 1991). In this chapter I explore one segment of that contest for space; the growth, development, and use of public housing in New Orleans. I argue that dominant structural forces aid and abet social isolation and thus contribute to the continued nurturing of urban poverty. I illustrate that an ideological symmetry exists between the contested space of public housing and public education (Garvin, 1994; Katz, 1975; Kozol, 1991; Miron, Lauria, & Dashner, 1994). First, I address some of the theoretical issues that surround the phenomenon of urban space and its social construction. This includes a detailed examination of Wilson's (1987) social isolation thesis, and ultimately, the phenomenon of social isolation as embedded in policy of housing segregation. Next, I look at the historical development of housing policy in the city of New Orleans and how the evolution of that policy illustrates the interactive relationship between human agency and social structure. Finally, I conclude this analysis by examining the linkage between social structure and children in public education and how that linkage may affect those children. The *Brown* decision clearly called attention to that linkage, yet, 40 years after it was rendered, I contend that the pernicious character of that linkage has yet to be abated.

A Theoretical Discussion

All cultures, as well as subcultures, function in particular patterns (Berger, 1977). The way those patterns reveal themselves and how they affect people are illustrated by the characteristics of the structural framework of any given society (Apple, 1990; Massey, Eggers, & Denton, 1989). The structural framework of a society includes a series of complex relationships that include the following elements: (a) the economic system, (b) social order, (c) educational system, and (d) government organizations, as well as the myths, rituals, and traditions that are particular to specific groups and specific regions (Foucault, 1972; Rothman, 1971; Seeman, 1983; Stinchcombe, 1968). These elements share two common characteristics; (a) because they are connected, they each contribute to a collective power that allows them to be stronger than if they existed unilaterally, and (b) the people who live and work inside each of the elements or systems are often locked into life situations that they cannot change by themselves (Apple, 1990; Stinchcombe, 1968). These situations are often determined, in part, by perception, or what Bourdieu (1977) calls "habitus." Bourdieu (1977) defines "habitus" as a system of lasting, transposable dispositions which, integrating past experiences, function at every moment as a matrix of perceptions, appreciations, and actions (pp. 82-83). Thus, habitus is a powerful part of the social construction of reality (Apple, 1990; Freire, 1990; Stinchcombe, 1968). And, notably, this notion of "every moment" is inclusive of place.

The Construction of Place

Place has a geographical context. That is, it is bounded by a specific geography; and, place has a social construction. The social construction of place includes (a) the relationship that exists between an individual and an immediate group of peers, (b) the relationship between an individual and society as a whole, and (c) the perception one holds of self as part of the dynamics of (a) and (b) (Bourdieu, 1977). One concept to be explored in this work is that the social construction of place can and is influenced by the geographical construction of space. Wilson (1987) contends that the relationship between geographical space and the social construction of place can result in "social isolation" under particular circumstances.

Wilson (1987) defines social isolation as lack of contact with individuals who represent the mainstream of society. This social isolation results from structural economic forces that physically separate people from jobs, as well as from the social mainstream, and people who are socially isolated in this context tend to be poor.

The highest concentrations of poverty are within the inner city (Goldsmith & Blakely, 1992; Massey et al., 1989; Wilson, 1987). And, within the inner city, public housing is the geographical place where the largest concentrations of people in poverty exist (Hirsch, 1983; Massey & Denton, 1993; Wilson, 1987).

It was Wilson's (1987) contention that those who are socially isolated need to exercise their individual and collective will, in order to be less isolated, and foster relationships with those who model behavior patterns which are more in compliance with mainstream cultural norms. This replication of middle- class social patterns, he would argue, would help facilitate the entrance of those who are isolated into mainstream society and mainstream societal activities (Wilson, 1987; 1992).

Wilson's notion of how to overcome social isolation fails to take into account the significant issues of race (Hacker, 1992;

Massey & Denton, 1993), class (Katz, 1993), educational attainment (Garvin & Miron, 1992), job availability, and of the evolving nature of the urban economic arena (Goldsmith & Blackall, 1992). Jobs, people, and private housing stock have disappeared from the inner city. The poor have been and continue to be bounded by reason of a socially constructed reality that would not allow them to leave. They were and are stymied by a lack of employment skills that fit into the new industrial technology and by a lack of fiscal resources that would allow them physically to move; both physical and social movement are stymied by issues of race and class. Thus, there is not this ease of movement that Wilson suggests from social isolation into social integration. The process is more complex and has far more barriers than his work would suggest. The economic structure wants employees with certain types of technical skills that the isolated do not have, since they have historically constituted an unskilled, manual labor force (Goldsmith & Blackall, 1992; Wilson, 1987); the educational structure asks allegiance to an urban school system that is ineffectual and inferior to the life needs of the students and the skills needed in today's economic arenas (Katz, 1975; Kozol, 1991); and the social structure has shown little encouragement for either assimilation or absorption of people of color (Massey & Denton, 1993). As a result, for the urban poor, mostly African American or Hispanic American, neither entry nor assimilation into the dominant societal structure occurs without encountering forces of resistance (Giroux & McLaren, 1989; Goldsmith & Blackall, 1992).

For many outside of the structures of the dominant society, particularly for people in poverty and people of color, there are separate societies at work, with different expectations, different resources available, and different expected outcomes (Goldsmith & Blackall, 1992; Hacker, 1992; Massey & Denton, 1993). There is an abundance of data that tells us the pay for people of color is less than for those from the dominant society, the access to educational facilities for people of color is more severely constrained than for others, and the barriers to employment are higher for those who are poor and of color (Goldsmith & Blackall, 1993; Hacker, 1992; Hirsch, 1983; Katz, 1987; Massey & Denton, 1993). All of these elements coalesce into a complex matrix which affects the lives of those who exist in those different and constrained societies (Garvin, Turner, & Miron, 1993; Katz, 1993; Kotlowitz, 1991; Massey & Denton, 1993; Ogbu, 1991, 1985).

In looking at the policies surrounding the siting of public housing in New Orleans, patterns begin to emerge which serve to illustrate the presence of larger structural forces, especially dominant culture views as expressed in the ideology of segregation, an ideology that impinges directly on the lives of the poor. Again, it is my hypothesis that dominant structural forces aid and abet social isolation and thus contribute to the continued nurturing of urban poverty. However, dominant structural forces are not neutral actors; rather they are the extension and result of a collective social will (Apple, 1990; Miron, Lauria, & Dashner, 1994). Thus, what exists is an interactive dynamic between one set of human agency decisions constraining another set of human agency decisions. The first, reflected in the structural forces at work in an ideological social order, by their very nature, limit the range of opportunity for the members of the second. The demise of the second group only serves to strengthen the ideology of the first group. Thus, the dynamic feeds back and forth on itself, with that ebbing and flowing seen as structure to human agency to structure. It is a living tug of war of social will.

The Historical and Social Context of the Inner City

The urban inner city and its companion, what has been problematically called the urban ghetto, is a creation of this last century, especially the second half (Hirsch, 1983). What has sprung up from this modern urban phenomenon are narrowly constrained geographical places that contain high concentrations of people who are almost exclusively African American, poor, and whose lives are controlled and patterned not only by the concrete and mortar environment where they live but by the social institutions that supposedly serve them.

Osofsky (1966), Zunz (1982), and Kusmer (1976) mark the early development of these urban inner city areas between the late 1800s through the early years of the Franklin Roosevelt presidency. This initial growth is marked by a demand in the industrial North for unskilled labor coupled with the beginnings of the mechanization of Southern agriculture (Lemann, 1991). The response was the migration of literally hundreds of thousands of African American in-country migrants to the Northern industrial cities of America looking for work. From 1890 to 1930, Chicago's African American population, for example, grew from 14,000 to more than 234,000 (Spear, 1967). Prior to those large increases, a certain racial and spatial harmony had existed in the larger Northern cities. Segregation had not yet taken hold and even among the social elite, the presence of African Americans was of little consequence (Zunz, 1982). However, with the dramatic increase in numbers, both social and spatial threats were felt and segregationist policies quickly became the norm rather than the exception (Kusmer, 1976). With the arithmetic increases in the African American population, constraints were placed on access to social and residential resources (Hirsch, 1983; Katz, 1975; Kusmer, 1976; Ploski & Williams, 1983; Zunz, 1982). More than 100 years later, those restraints, while now considered illegal, continue to be felt (Goldsmith & Blackall, 1992; Massey & Denton, 1993).

The Problems of African American Assimilation

While the large in-country migration wave was in effect washing over the industrial cities, a second wave from Europe was also depositing thousands of new immigrants into those same cities. They, too, were poor and with marginal labor skills. However, their stay within these impoverished inner city areas of U.S. cities was but transitory as they assimilated and absorbed quickly into American culture (Hirsch, 1983). Possessed of the same labor skills, having the same desires, Southern African Americans were neither absorbed nor assimilated. Institutional, governmental, and individual actions, willful in their intent and purpose, came together not only to deny access but to set aside limited geographical space in which only African Americans were to reside (Massey & Denton, 1993; Spain, 1993).

Prior to the beginning of this large migration into the industrial cities, less than 13% of African Americans lived in large urban areas. In the almost 100 years that have followed, that number has dramatically turned and by the 1980s, only 1% of the more than 26 million African Americans in this country live in rural areas. Being African American and living in America had become largely an urban phenomenon (Ploski & Williams, 1983).

However, even with large increases in population and with several cities showing African American majority population bases by the 1960s and 1970s, there was little significant change in the social and spatial status for poor African Americans. This group, with marginal labor skills and marginal educational experiences, continued to be compressed into smaller and smaller space with fewer and fewer available resources (Hacker, 1992; Spain, 1993; Wilson, 1987). The advent of the Civil Rights movement changed the access to political power for some. However, erosion continued to take place in economic terms (Goldsmith & Blackall, 1992; Massey & Denton, 1993).

The Residential Displacement of African Americans

While the case can be made that a portion of the residential clustering of any immigrant group is partially voluntary, little evidence exists to suggest that African Americans had any range of choice on where to live and who their neighbors might be (Hirsch, 1983). These choices were limited by early Jim Crow legislation, later by deed and covenant restrictions of real estate transfers, federal mortgage guidelines, and federal and state guidelines on public housing. All of this served to siphon off choice and channel African American residency to very particular locales. One of these locales was public housing, which was not just an alternative site for many inner city African Americans — it increasingly became the only place to live.

This channeling of a large portion of a city's population into geographically bounded housing developments that were massive in scope and size, occurred as two other phenomena blossomed. The first was the large scale exodus of the white population from the city to the suburbs. It was not only an exodus of human resources but also of fiscal resources (Gottdiener, 1985; Wilson, 1987). As these individuals left, following jobs and an emerging suburban housing market, the city's tax base dwindled. Thus, fewer fiscal resources existed for the growing social needs of an ever increasing poor population, which was predominantly African American and living in public housing developments. The second phenomenon was in time frame coupled to the first, a technological shift in the workplace. Manufacturing in the classical sense was rapidly disappearing and with its demise so too went the demand for large pools of unskilled labor (Goldsmith & Blackall, 1992; Wilson, 1987).

At a time when increasing resources were needed to bridge the transition from a manufacturing to a technological workplace, for the urban poor those resources were, in fact, diminishing. Large concentrations of population, African American almost in its entirety, trapped in ghetto environments and often in public housing developments, were facing rapidly decreasing employment opportunities, and fewer resources by which to take advantage of the few opportunities that remained. Formed by government policies of residential space, and bracketed by a global economic shift to technology, the inner city ghetto now sits as a living monument to this country's longest historical social inequity. New Orleans tells that story in a very specific way.

New Orleans, Jim Crow, and the Color Line

New Orleans is the largest city in the state of Louisiana with a population of approximately 500,000 people. Sixty-three percent (63%) of the New Orleans population is African American, with Hispanic Americans making up 3.4% of the population and Asians 1.3%. The remainder of the population is white, about 32% (U.S. Census, 1990). Over one-fourth of all the city's households (26.7%) live at or below the poverty level (Mayor's Office, 1992). Approximately 55,000, 12% of the city's total population, live in public housing, and almost all of them are African American (Mayor's Office, 1992).

The early 20th century development of a housing policy in New Orleans was and continues to be racial in nature and intent (Garvin, 1994; Mahoney, 1985). This is not to say that New Orleans was unique as a Southern city in this regard or unique as a city without reference to its geographical location (Schermer, 1968). Cities in general have always tended to be places where the constraints of space and the presence of capital have produced inequities in the human environment (Harvey, 1989; Katznelson, 1985).

As a city, and a city nestled within the home region of Jim Crow, New Orleans was capable of its own production of inequities in human relationships. Restrictions on real estate exchanges between the races are illustrated by articles which ran in the New Orleans newspaper in the early 1920s:

> Bill to Restrict Negro Buildings is Introduced
> An ordinance to regulate the settlement of Negroes in white neighborhoods, and of whites in Negro neighborhoods carrying out the provisions of ACT 118 or (sic) 1924 . . . prohibits issuance of building certificates to

Negroes desiring to build in white neighborhoods.
                    Times Picayune Sept. 10, 1924 p. 7

Negroes Barred from Building
Too Near Whites
It required less than 10 seconds yesterday for
the commission council to adopt an ordinance
on final passage preventing construction of
Negro homes in white communities. "You
may be sure that not only myself but every
other mother of white children in New Orleans
sincerely appreciates this restriction that will
prevent Negro children from coming into our
communities and mixing with our children,"
Mrs. Stephens said.   The ordinance was
adopted under Act 118 of the Louisiana Legislature which grants cities of 10,000 or more
the right to enact such restrictions.
                Times Picayune Sept. 17, 1924, p.14

The issue of social place as tied to specific geographical
space was so important, it too was spelled out:

"Whites to Test Segregation Act"
White community and black community are
defined to "embrace every residence fronting
on either side of any street within 300 feet of
the location of the property involved, measured
along the middle of the street in any and all
directions.
                Times Picayune Sept. 19, 1924 p.1 & p. 9

White Resistance and Public Policy
Obviously there was strong acceptance by the white community of New Orleans to the so-called color line. That acceptance
was evident in the policies of residential segregation and these
same ideological policies surrounded the construction of public
housing developments. Public housing in New Orleans was a
study in dualism, one set of public housing for whites and one set
of public housing for African Americans, with different quality of

life standards for each (Mahoney, 1985). For those few African American residents in the city who did own their own homes, they were often forced from their property, seeing their homes razed in order to make room for construction of public housing developments (Neighborhood Profiles Project, 1980). The excuses to take those private properties always seems to be tied to issues other than race:

> Van of 5,000 Local Families Move into
> Low Rent Projects
> A few years earlier a social survey revealed that because of crowded and unsanitary conditions and because of the general prevalence of nonweatherproof houses among low-income families in New Orleans, disease was taking a large toll of persons living under such conditions, especially among the Negro population.
> *Times Picayune*, Jan 15, 1941, Sec. 3, p. 2

In this quotation, prevention of disease was given as the reason for razing owner-occupied housing, yet unsanitary conditions and disease were specifically tied to race, that is, the African American population. The entire matter of overcrowding and unsanitary conditions within areas occupied by African Americans was used to justify the need for tearing down African American neighborhoods and erecting public housing in their place.

New Orleans, Public Housing, and Federal Policy

This association between public housing, disease, and the early history of the ideology of public housing policy in New Orleans, specifically moving working-class African American families into the developments, closely tracks the national development of public housing policy. Federal policymakers were concerned not to have public housing associated with those who were on relief (Katz, 1987; Spain, 1993). Public housing was for the temporarily unfortunate, not for those contaminated with the twin diseases of race and poverty. This point was made clear to the local housing authority administrators in the National Association of Housing Officials' (NAHO) 1939 Manual from Early Experience:

> The welfare agencies and the local housing authority should work out some limit to the number or percent of

relief or WPA families that will be accommodated in a public housing development . . . . There are both physical and psychological dangers in allowing a public housing project to become tenanted predominantly with recipients of public assistance . . . the concentration of public welfare families in a housing project would immediately place a brand upon the development and would prevent the establishment of a normal community representing various income levels and normal occupations. (HANO, 1939: p.V21–22)

In New Orleans and in Louisiana, public housing was initially perceived in the same manner. In fact, the Louisiana State Housing Commission (LSHC) was activated in 1921 based on "great need for more units where the *laboring* class live (LSHC minutes). Occupancy in public housing was to be limited to "responsible tenants, chosen in order that every family accepted for consideration is capable of paying the rent and has a satisfactory character (LSHC minutes). Additionally, the first criterion of eligibility for public housing favored married couples; the George-Healey Act of 1936 specified that public housing should be available only to *families* who lacked sufficient income to afford decent, safe housing in the private market (USHA, 1939). The ideal, eligible tenant family was succinctly described in the 1938 pamphlet put out by the United States Housing Authority (USHA):

The immediate purpose of public housing is to raise the living standards of typical employed families of very low income, who are independent and self-supporting . . . . Public housing is designed to improve the conditions of millions of working families who have reasonably steady jobs and reasonably steady but inadequate earnings. (USHA, 1939)

While policymakers were making it clear for whom public housing was to be built, they also were making it clear *where* this housing should be built. While site selection of federally financed housing developments was left to local authorities by the legislation of 1935, the National Housing Agency of the Federal Public Housing Authority released a document entitled "Public Housing Design" (1946) that was intended to surreptitiously mandate site-selection guidelines (Spain, 1993). Its initial chapter maintained that successful developments would be built near transportation routes, shopping, schools, churches, and medical facilities. It contained an example of a neighborhood map which showed the "reasonable distance" to such services and facilities. The intent of the document was to illustrate the elements federal officials felt were needed to create both neighborhood and a way to ensure that the new neighborhood would be part of the overall community; and this assistance was being offered in an attempt to prevent public housing from degenerating into slums (National Housing Act, 1946).

Reasonable distances were recommended as follows: for public transit stops, one quarter to three quarters of a mile away; the same distance was used for shopping, libraries, and churches. Grade schools were to be no more than one half mile away and high schools no more than one mile. Hospitals were to be within a half hour commute by public transit. In New Orleans these guidelines were met when the local housing authority selected the location for the first two public housing developments, St. Thomas and Magnolia.

These initial developments were located near the central core of the city and, as a result, were well within the guidelines since many of the services and facilities were clustered near that core. In fact, the first six housing developments all met these benchmarks: St. Thomas, occupied in 1941, followed in that same year by Magnolia, Iberville, Lafitte, and Calliope. The St. Bernard complex was occupied in 1942, and the Florida site in 1946.

The Racially Segregated Housing Developments

African American and white low income working families were racially segregated by housing developments: St. Thomas and Iberville for whites; and Florida, Calliope, Magnolia, and St. Bernard for African Americans (HANO minutes, 1938, 1939). No more than 20% of tenants could be drawn from each of five different employment categories as designated by the housing authority; (a) domestic workers, (b) those in the shipping industry, (c) the automobile industry, in this instance, automobile dealerships, (d) miscellaneous, and (e) no more than 20% could be assigned to families on relief (HANO, 1940 minutes).

St. Thomas and Magnolia, located in what New Orleanians describe as "uptown," were built to replace slum housing that was decayed housing stock previously occupied by African American families (Carter, 1941). Iberville and Lafitte were just off the main center-city thoroughfare, Canal Street, and thus were located in the very heart of the city. While the African American projects were well thought of by the tenants who initially occupied them, it was also clear that the two white projects had better access to paved streets than any of the African American projects enjoyed and were less isolated from the rest of the community (HANO, 1941 minutes). In a time when a significant number of people still walked from home to transit stops, having a paved street was no small blessing, especially in a rainy, sub-tropical climate like that of New Orleans. That this is noted without comment in the housing authority's minutes is an indication of both racial status and racial priority. Nonetheless, each of the early developments, both African American and white, was well received. The one exception was St. Bernard, which was a development built for African Americans. Built away from the center of the city and away from neighborhoods, St. Bernard was not only isolated geographically, it was also isolated from almost all facilities and services. The closest bus stop was over a mile away, and in a decision which still stands without recorded explanation, all telephone service in the project, which consisted of a bank of pay telephones in a courtyard, was turned off at night (Mahoney, 1985).

Unfortunately, St. Bernard's exception to the rule was short lived. A number of reasons appear to have contributed to this change. Public housing surfaced out of pressures wrought by the Depression and from policy coming out of the New Deal. Many of the developments were just opening with the beginning of the Second World War. The wartime economy changed the population dynamics in a number of significant ways. Skilled and unskilled workers were able to find full employment and a general air of prosperity raised personal levels of ambition and hope in almost every tenant within the developments.

But the jobs attracted thousands of people from outside the city as well. The 1940 and 1950 U.S. Census data indicated that between 1940 and 1950, the white population of New Orleans grew 14%, climbing by 47,311 new people (U.S. Census, 1940, 1950). The non-white population rose approximately 23% or by 33,597 people (U.S. Census). But wars and wartime economies do not go on forever. While the boom had created economic prosperity across all class and racial lines, by the war's end, African Americans were still generally confined to the most unskilled jobs. According to the 1950 Census, household workers and laborers were the largest employment categories among the African American population. Additionally, as servicemen returned from the war looking for work, employers preferred whites either for new openings or to move back into positions held by others (African Americans) while they were away (Northrup & Rowan, 1970; Ploski & Williams, 1983; Thayer & Lorber, 1973). The result was that for many African Americans, the end of the war meant the end of the boom and in the ensuing years that followed, African American unemployment rose dramatically, increasing almost tenfold (Northrup & Rowan, 1970; Ploski & Williams, 1983; Thayer & Lorber, 1973).

For many African American families, public housing after World War II represented the best available housing for both the employed and unemployed. It was at this juncture that the character of public housing began to change. Public housing and welfare were social service policies that were developed to be solutions to temporary circumstances. Neither was supposedly built to last (Spain, 1993). But a certain duality was at work within the African American experience.

For white tenants who lived in New Orleans's public housing, the post-war boom afforded them the opportunity to find and buy private homes, which they did. During the final days of World War II, the white vacancy rate in St. Thomas and Iberville was almost double that of the vacancy rate in the African American developments (HANO, 1943–44 Report). While the units were left vacant in the white projects, African American projects had long waiting lists for those looking for housing (Thayer, 1978). Without redress to the private housing market, African Americans had no place to turn but to public housing. The demand to get into the facilities grew ever larger and, at one point in 1949, HANO had 46,000 African American families on the waiting list (HANO, 1949 Report). Meanwhile, the vacancies continued to climb in the white developments. The white vacancy problem became so acute that HANO sent out a mass mailing to the white community encouraging them to investigate the benefits of public housing (HANO, 1951 Report). It had little effect. However, what was quite clear was that whites held a higher status in the access to all housing resources. Both public policymaking and its implementation created two different societies and two different citizenships.

As a result of the war and high rates of employment for whites and African Americans, money was available for housing.

Mortgages from private lenders for housing were insured by the Federal Housing Administration (FHA). During this time, the FHA, however, advocated zoning and deed restrictions to bar certain classifications of what they considered to be undesirable people. Racial minorities were in those categories and often found themselves described as nuisances because of their perceived impact on a residential area (Federal Public Housing Authority, 1946). As a result, even those African Americans with fiscal resources had a hard time gaining access to housing in the private market (Massey & Denton, 1993; Spain, 1993).

As Mahoney (1985) suggests, it would be hard to estimate the power and human impact given the legitimation of racialized lending and appraisal policies: " . . . the refusal to lend *where* blacks live has a *more sweeping impact* than the refusal to make loans *to* blacks" (p.1259). This "where" was a significant issue, for if you will recall the earlier newspaper accounts, laws were still on the books which made it illegal for African Americans to purchase housing stock held by whites in New Orleans. In this instance, place becomes a person, for access to place is denied through the person. The dominant society was white; those aspiring to enter that society who were not white were literally placed elsewhere.

Geography, Resources, and Inequity

This inequity of resource distribution by race continued. In 1956, the Desire Housing Development opened and became the home for 14,000 people, most of whom were children, all of whom were African American (HANO, 1958 Report). The location of the Desire Development, as well as the quality of its construction, continued to reinforce the impression of an ideology of segregationist policies from both local and federal government organizations. At the time it was under construction, a series of articles appeared in the local newspaper detailing a number of questionable construction practices. Those accounts told of minimal performance standards, the use of materials of questionable quality, below average workmanship and of foundations pulling away from the walls of new buildings. Nonetheless, HUD accepted the buildings as they were, and residents were moved into the buildings (*Times-Picayune*, April 16, 1956).

Previously, and noting the exception of St. Bernard, public housing developments in New Orleans had been built around the central core of the city. The Desire Housing Development marked a post-World War II departure from that policy. Built as the last locally federally funded project from the 1949 Housing Act, the Desire Development sits between two canals and two sets of railroad tracks. It is isolated both geographically and by a lack of infrastructure. For a long period of time, a single road, unpaved for years, entered the complex of 262 buildings that contains 1,860 living units. That road, and the roads which feed into it, cross two railroad tracks, and it is the blockage of these tracks by the trains that results in Desire and its inhabitants being cut off for hours at a time from the rest of the world while they wait for the tracks to clear (Mahoney, 1985; Rocque, 1993).

Because of poor construction, noted from the date of its opening, the Desire Development has been plagued with sewage problems, drainage problems, doors falling off, foundations sinking, and other structural malaise (Times Picayune, 1956). Additionally, Desire's location transgressed every suggested federal mandate about reasonable distance from facilities and services. This was the policy response for African Americans who needed housing while the white developments of St. Thomas and Iberville grew increasingly vacant.

Returning to Bourdieu's (1977) concept of habitus and the social construction of reality, the context of the living environment for African Americans in the city of New Orleans as seen in the material that has just been reviewed, had and continues to have the following characteristics:

1. Races were segregated, both by law and by the attitudes of those in the dominant host society.

2. Where those members of each race could live and work was not equal, even if it were separate.

3. Even with the passage of significant social legislation, starting in the 1960s, there exist separate and unequal worlds for those who are poor and of color and for those who are white.

The racial concentration seen in public housing in New Orleans, and elsewhere, was inevitable; it was built into the African American community through the use of segregation policies, housing and otherwise (Garvin, 1994; Mahoney, 1985, 1990; Massey & Denton, 1993). In looking for answers as to why African American poverty endures, maybe we have to look no further than the historical constraints of segregation as a reflection of social ideology and what it has wrought. Without places to live, without jobs to work, poverty was also inevitable. Poverty sets off a series of ancillary changes in both the social and economic composition of communities (Massey & Denton, 1993). Those changes are elucidated quite clearly by Massey and Denton (1993):

> Deleterious conditions such as falling retail demand, increasing residential abandonment, rising crime, spreading disorder, increasing welfare dependency, growing family disruption and rising educational failure are all concentrated simultaneously by raising the rate of poverty under the regime of high segregation. (p. 146)

Certainly, while New Orleans is a Southern city, its experience is not unique because of its Southern location. Boston, Cincinnati, Baltimore, and Pittsburgh have remarkably parallel scenarios (Schermer, 1964, 1965, 1966). In each of these cities, African Americans and minorities have faced similar housing and employment obstacles. In each of these cities, housing developments have been sited where they are away from residential neighborhoods or where they are naturally bounded by rivers, highways, or large expanses of vacant land (Spain, 1993). Why all of this occurred may be best summed up by Hirsch's (1983) statement about the "second ghetto" and its development in Chicago:

> . . . . the second ghetto has a history of its own. Born of the struggle between planners and politicians, racists and liberals, ethnics and institutions, it was the product of all: none could have done it alone. (p. 258)

Public Housing, Schools, Children, and Social Isolation

While technically illegal, the continued social construction of segregation of poor people of color exacts a price, a price from both the segregated and those who would segregate them. In the city of New Orleans, 55,000 individuals live in public housing, almost all (99%) of whom are African American. Of that number, almost 28,000 are school-age children. The prior discussion was concerned with the development of an area that is physically isolated and the subsequent impact of that isolation on the lives of the residents. But what of other social institutions, in particular schools, that have been encapsulated within these socially constructed zones of isolation, and more importantly, what may be the impact of these isolationist policies on the children who live in public housing and who attend these schools?

Recent research would suggest that the academic performance of children is related to both cognitive skills and motivational beliefs (Borkowski, Johnston, & Reid, 1986). Is there some relationship between the ideology of segregation as manifested in this environment of social isolation and the motivational beliefs of these children? If so, is this linkage important? Found in the research by Borkowski, Johnston, and Reid (1986), and later again by Garvin, Turner, and Miron (1993), as well as Little, Oettingen, Linderberger, and Baltes (1994), motivational beliefs appear to be related to academic success or failure. Inappropriate beliefs may inhibit a child's ability to take advantage of learning situations, and then lead to poor academic performance. The source of that inhibited ability may be a mismatch between the child's belief and the beliefs embedded within the curriculum to which the child is subjected. My aim in this section is to illustrate some of those potential sources creating that mismatch by:

1. Describing the control beliefs of students from a cross section of schools within the city of New Orleans, including the children from a school located in the midst of a public housing development.

2. Measuring the relationship of those control beliefs to academic achievement.

3. Determining if there is a difference in control beliefs by *where* the children live.

Subjects

Five hundred ninety-one (591) students from the third through the sixth grades in four urban schools within the city of New Orleans were surveyed in 1992 and 1993. The average age was 10.5 years. The sample consisted of 94% African Americans, 2% European Americans, 3% Asian Americans, and 1% Mexican Americans. The four schools consisted primarily of children from low income families, but varied to the extent of poverty and the type of family housing represented. Schools 1 and 2 drew from lower-middle-class homes as well as families living in Section 8 housing. Section 8 housing is a federal program where families live in and rent single family dwellings with the rent being subsidized by the government. Of the students from schools 1 and 2, 49% and 52%, respectively were on free lunch. The Federal Department of Agriculture (FDA) subsidizes the cost of lunch for children in public schools based on the family's level of income.

Any child whose lunch is free is usually in a family whose income is below the poverty level. School 3 drew its student population exclusively from a public housing development, all of whom were African American. Ninety-nine percent (99%) of those students were on free lunch. School 4 had a student population that came from Section 8 housing and a public housing complex. Of those students, 76% were on free lunch.

The Student's Perception of Control Questionnaire (SPOCQ) (Wellborn, Connell, & Skinner, 1989) was administered to the students. This scale was selected because of the three types of beliefs that it measures:

1. Control Beliefs (CON) — the belief in one's ability to control outcomes.

2. Strategy Beliefs (ST) — the means viewed as important in controlling outcomes.

3. Capacity Beliefs (CP) — the student's perception of their own access to strategies.

School 3 has markedly diminished SPOCQ scores (See Table 1). It appears that the students in school 3 might be different in their attitudes about themselves, their attitudes about their ability to learn and in their capacity to believe that they control their own lives.

Table 1
Across Gender MAXCON - School Effect

School	Mean	Sig of F
1	38.336	<.001
2	35.541	<.001
3	24.611	<.001
4	30.931	<.001

A letter was sent home initially with each of the students asking permission not only for the children to participate in the questionnaire/survey but also asking permission from the parents to examine the child's academic records as well as any other information in their files that may prove to be helpful in under-standing the role of place in this data analysis. Two hundred forty-eight (248) parents responded in the positive, giving permission to have access to the children's files.

Two hundred forty-five (245) individual records were ultimately examined and the following information was gathered from each of those files:

1. Place of residence.

2. Family income, measured by whether a child is on free or reduced lunch - children are eligible for either free or reduced status based on reported family income. As a result, whatever classification a child falls into serves as an indicator of family income levels.

3. Whether a child is in a family unit with two parents or a single parent.

4. Scoring on standardized achievement tests, specifically the California Achievement Tests.

5. Absenteeism rates for each student.

6. Behavior grades.

A preliminary examination of that second wave of analysis looked at the relationship of the SPOCQ to those students in the sample who were on free lunch. Free lunch was the indicator used to delineate income levels of each student's family. Table 2 indicates that school 3, which had the highest percentage of students on free lunch, also had the lowest mean scores on the SPOCQ:

Table 2
SPOCQ Score by School

School	% Free Lunch	SPOCQ
1	49	36.9
2	52	34.3
3	99	25.5
4	76	33.3

The presence of a high percentage of children on free lunch was used as a marker for low income populations. The students at school 3 were also from a particular place, a public housing development, and that place was populated by a high percentage of poor people. This apparently is some indication of the impact of the density of poverty that was discussed by Wilson (1987), Massey and Denton (1993), and Goldsmith and Blackall (1992). Massey and Denton (1993), in particular, argue that segregationist housing policies tend to concentrate poverty populations and the worse social effects of poverty. The next part of the analysis was to determine how well the SPOCQ instrument and its measurements could correlate to academic achievement, the gender of the student, whether or not the student was from a single parent home, absences, latenesses, behavior grades, and family income. This was a multiple regression analysis with the dependent variable being achievement and the predictors being the SPOCQ, absences, free lunch, latenesses, behavior grades, and parental status. That initial analysis, on the reduced sample of 245 students where permission had been granted by the parents, was done by looking at all of those factors against data found in the standardized achievement tests used by the Orleans Parish Public School System. In this particular instance, that test was the California Achievement Test. The California Achievement Test is given in two sections, reading and math. In each of those, the SPOCQ emerged as the strongest predictor of those scores (Table 3 and Table 4).

Table 3
California Achievement Test - Reading

Variable	% Variance	F	Sig F
SPOCQ	16.2	29.66	.000
Absences	7.2	23.76	.000
Free Lunch	5.0	19.96	.000
Behavior	2.8	17.08	.000

Table 4
California Achievement Test - Math

Variable	% Variance	F	Sig F
SPOCQ	16.4	30.19	.000
Absences	6.6	22.93	.000
Free Lunch	4.0	18.96	.000
Behavior	2.8	16.33	.000

The same analysis was done again, but instead of standard-ized achievement tests, the grades of the students were used. In this instance, the SPOCQ was found to be a more robust predictor, accounting for almost 31% of the variance (Table 5 and Table 6). No other factor approached this figure other than behavior. What was not found to be significant was free lunch status, absences, latenesses, or whether the child came from a single parent home.

Table 5
School Grades - Reading

Variable	% Variance	F	Sig F
SPOCQ	30.7	101.12	.000
Behavior	13.0	88.29	.000

Table 6
School Grades - Math

Variable	% Variance	F	Sig F
SPOCQ	28.9	92.75	.000
Behavior	8.3	67.33	.000

At this juncture, a decision was made to narrow the focus of the analysis. The population sample of all the children (245) whose parents had given permission to gather the data on grades, absences, and test scores had been considered in all of the previous analyses. What was clear from an examination of those outcomes was that school, or where the school was located, appeared to be a predominant factor in the SPOCQ scores; the school which had the lowest mean SPOCQ scores had the highest percentage of children on free lunch, and that the SPOCQ instrument was a strong predictor of academic achievement within this sample population.

Was it possible that school 3 was lowest simply because it had more poor students and not because of place or isolation? Although this cannot be ruled out completely, an attempt was made to address that issue. SPOCQ scores were analyzed for only the children on free lunch. This does not completely equate for a measure of the extent of poverty, but it does include only those students below the established federal guidelines for the poverty level. If income is the issue, the place of school should no longer be significant. Across this part of the sample population 202 students were on free lunch and they became the study group for this next phase of the analysis.

When examining all the SPOCQ scales in an aggregate measure, MAXCON, both strategy and capacity, the students of school 3 showed a much lower SPOCQ mean than any of the other schools (Table 7):

Table 7
MAXCON (all factors together)

F	Sig. of F	School	Mean	SD	N
3.46	<.05	1	38.87	11.81	29
		2	31.77	20.36	33
		3	24.97	16.32	72
		4	30.66	19.67	78

The data indicate that the children in school 3 have a diminished capacity of belief in their ability to control their lives and to effect strategies that they consider important for academic success. Again, school 3 is the only school whose physical location is in the middle of a public housing development. While there are a vast array of factors that may account for these numerical findings, the findings themselves warrant attention and reflection, as well as further study.

The statistics, these numbers, and data represent real people, real children. It appears that the social construction of space and of construction of social place has created a dynamic that plays a role in how these children see themselves, in how these children see the world and how these children perform in an academic setting. That setting, however, is marginalized. Built almost 20 years ago, specifically for the children who lived in this public housing development, the school has a playground that consists only of a large slab of asphalt, surrounded by a chain link fence.

There is not any playground equipment, no slides, no swings and there has not been any playground equipment for these children since the day it opened. None of the classrooms are air-conditioned, and in the warmer months, temperature inside the building often exceeds 120 degrees. No funds are budgeted for air conditioning these facilities. The faculty, the staff, the children of this school, and all the tenants of the public housing development are African American and poor. In an era that has seen the advent of desegregation and supposedly fostered assimilation, these children are nonetheless segregated and isolated. The development in which these children live and the school which they attend, as a physical infrastructure that reflects a dominant social structure, is little more than a worn, outdated, and crumbling warehouse, a holding facility.

Conclusion

In this chapter I have looked at the institutions of public housing and public education as a collective social lens through which to look at the effects of the *Brown* decision four decades after it was rendered. The images are neither heartening nor hopeful. In both cases, the behavior of those who fund, control, and provide policy for those institutions are problematic for the very people they are meant to serve — the poor and their children. It is clear that the social context of where and how people live has a dramatic impact of where and how they are schooled, what they are taught, and demonstrates who has power and who does not. The *Brown* decision was viewed as a rebirth of the American dream for those who had failed to have been given the opportunity to live that dream. Now, that dream seems to have nightmarish qualities.

In city after city, under the guise of any number of programs, urban renewal, the Great Society et al., poor African Americans have been put aside and warehoused in public housing developments (Katz, 1993; Peterson, 1976; Teaford, 1990). Neither accidental in its creation nor in its enduring nature, this environment of poverty is a foundation built from purposeful forces. The sites of these developments increasingly have a uniformity to them: geographical (horizontal or vertical) isolation, high population densities, specific ethnic composition, and a lack of easy access to public services and facilities (Hirsch, 1983).

The resulting behavioral patterns from living in such conditions are now being described in terms of pathologies (Crane, 1991), as if some form of a strange and dreaded disease has suddenly been caught. In essence, a social leprosy and leprosarium have come to the forefront — the residents of and the phenomenon of public housing. The residents of public housing have become the outcasts with the places were they live and where they are schooled, the land of the outcasts.

The unfortunate and bitter truth is that what we have seen in this chapter about public housing and its residents reflects all too accurately the attitude that so many have about the poor. It is an attitude that wants the poor to be the poor, that wants the poor to be elsewhere, and it is an attitude that gives minimal benefits for assistance. With large urban school systems becoming the academic home for the urban poor, there exists a similar and parallel attitude about urban public education — keep the poor kids in the poor schools in the poor neighborhoods and fund those schools with minimal dollars (Kozol, 1991).

The weight of being in this land of outcasts seems to be falling on the shoulders of those most innocent in any society, the children. Now, 40 years after the *Brown* decision, a decision meant to effect a change for the betterment of children, there is little room to be encouraged. While legislating desegregation, the work of deconstructing the social apparatus of segregation was never carried out. Manifesting itself in the policies of public housing, the foreboding specter of this blatant inhumanity is invasive, cancerous, ravaging, and devastating the appendaged social institutions of schools and the disregarded children who attend them. While Hirsch (1983) eloquently claims we must all bear responsibility, there is little doubt we all must bear the shame.

References

Andrews, H. F. (1987). The effect of neighborhood social mix on adolescent's social networks and recreational activities. *Urban Studies, 23*, 501–571.

Apple, M. W. (1990). *Ideology and curriculum.* New York: Routledge.

Berger, P., & Neuhaus, J. (1977). *To empower people.* Washington, DC: American Enterprise Institute.

Borkowski, J. G., Johnston. M. B., & Reid, M. M. (1986). Metacognition, motivation and the transfer of control processes. In

S.J. Ceci (Ed.), *Handbook of cognitive, social and neuro-pyschological aspects of learning disabilities.* Hillsdale, NJ: Erlbaum.

Bourdieu, P. (1977). *Outline of a theory of practice.* Cambridge: Cambridge University Press.

Carter, S. (1941). *Metropolitan New Orleans: A survey of land use, real property, low income housing.* Baton Rouge, LA: Department of Public Welfare, State of Louisiana.

Crane, J. (1991). The epidemic theory of ghettos and neighbor hood effects on dropping out and teenage childbearing. *American Journal of Sociology, 96*(5), 1226–1259.

Davis. B., & McCaul, E. (1991). *The emerging crisis: Current and projected status of children in the United States.* Institute for the Study of At-Risk Students, University of Maine.

Foucault, M. (1972). *The archaeology of knowledge.* New York: Pantheon.

Freire, P. (1990). *Pedagogy of the oppressed.* New York: Continuum Publishing Company.

Garvin, J. R. (1994). Poverty, social isolation and children - gifts of the inner-city to the 21st century. In F. Moulaert (Ed.), *Cities, enterprises and society on the eve of the 21st Century.* Lille, France.

Garvin, J. R., Turner, L. A., & Miron, L. M. (1993). *Belief, culture and curriculum.* Paper presented at the annual meeting of the American Educational Research Association, Atlanta, GA.

Giroux. H., & McLaren P. (1989). *Critical pedagogy, the state and cultural struggle.* Albany, NY: State University of New York Press.

Goldsmith, W. W., & Blackall, E. J. (1992). *Separate societies: Poverty and inequality in U.S. cities.* Philadelphia: Temple University Press.

Gottdiener, M. (1985). *The social production of urban space.* Austin, TX: University of Texas Press.

Hacker, A. (1992). *Two nations: Black and white, separate, hostile, unequal.* New York: Ballatine Books.

Harvey, D. (1989). *The urban experience.* Oxford: Basil Blackwell.

Hirsch, A. R. (1983). *Making the second ghetto: Race and housing in Chicago, 1940–1960.* New York: Cambridge University Press.

Housing Authority of New Orleans, minutes from board meeting, Jan 20, 1941, pp. 101–104.

Housing Authority of New Orleans, minutes from board meeting, Jan–June, 1939, pp. 137–373, 397, 565.

Housing Authority of New Orleans, (1938). Minute books.

Housing Authority of New Orleans, (1939). Minute books.

Housing Authority of New Orleans, (1940). Minute books.

Housing Authority of New Orleans, (1941). Minute books.

Housing Authority of New Orleans, (1944). *1943–44 Report*, New Orleans.

Housing Authority of New Orleans, (1950). *1949 Report*, New Orleans.

Housing Authority of New Orleans, (1952). *1951 Report*, New Orleans.

Katz, M. B. (1975). *Class, bureaucracy and school: The illusion of educational change in America* (Expanded ed.). New York: Praeger Publishers.

Katz, M. B. (1987). *In the shadow of the poorhouse: A history of poverty in America.* Philadelphia: University of Pennsylvania Press.

Katz, M. B. (Ed.). (1993). *The "underclass debate."* Princeton, NJ: Princeton University Press.

Katznelson, I. (1985). *Schooling for all: Class, race, and the declining of the American ideal.* New York: Basic Books.

Kotlowitz, A. (1991). *There are no children here.* New York: Doubleday.

Kozol, J. (1991). *Savage inequalities: Children in America's schools.* New York: Crown Publishing.

Kusmer, K. L. (1976). *A ghetto takes shape: Black Cleveland, 1870–1930.* Urbana, IL: University of Illinois Press.

Lemann, N. (1991). *The promised land.* New York: Knopf Publishing Company.

Little, T., Oettingen, G., Linderberger, U., & Baltes, P. (1994). Causality, agency, and control beliefs in East versus West Berlin children: A natural experiment on the role of content. *Journal of Personality and Social Psychology, 66*(3), 579–595.

Louisiana State Housing Commission. (1921). Minute book No. 1.

Mahoney, M. (1985). *The changing nature of public housing in New Orleans: 1930–1974.* Unpublished master's thesis, Tulane University, New Orleans, LA.

Mahoney, M. (1990). Law and racial geography: Public housing and the economy in New Orleans. *Stanford Law Review, 42,* 1251–1290.

Massey, D. S., & Denton, N. A. (1993). *American apartheid: Segregation and the making of the underclass.* Cambridge, MA: Harvard University Press.

Massey, D. S., Eggers, M. L., & Denton, N. (1989). *Disen tangling the causes of concentrated poverty.* Paper presented at The William Julius Wilson Conference on The Truly Disadvantaged, Chicago, IL.

Mayor's Office. (1992, March). [Interview with Mayor of New Orleans and Staff].

Miron, L. (1991). The dialectics of school leadership: Post structural implications. *Organizational Theory Dialogue,* Fall, 1–5.

Miron, L., & Garvin, J. (1992). *Meeting national goals through community development.* Paper presented to the annual meeting of the National Association of Elementary School Principals, New Orleans, LA.

Miron, L., Lauria M., & Dasher, D. J. (1994). *Student resistance to the entrepreneurial coalition's drive for ideological hegemony.* DURPS Working Paper No. 23. New Orleans, LA: University of New Orleans.

National Housing Agency. (1946). *Public housing design.* Washington, DC: Federal Public Housing Authority.

Neighborhood Profiles Project. (1980). New Orleans: Office of the Mayor, City of New Orleans.

Northrup, H., & Rowan, R. (1970). *Negro employment in Southern industry.* Philadelphia: University of Pennsylvania.

Ogbu, J. U. (1985). Cultural-ecological influences on minority education. *Language Arts, 62*(8), 860–869.

Ogbu, J. U. (1991). Minority status and literacy in comparative perspective. In S. R. Graubard (Eds.), *Literacy: An overview by 14 experts.* New York: Hill and Wang.

Osofsky, G. (1966). *Harlem, the making of a ghetto: Negro New York, 1890–1930.* New York: Harper and Row.

Peterson, P. (1976). *School politics Chicago style.* Chicago: University of Chicago Press.

Ploski, H., & Williams, J. (1983). *The Negro almanac: A reference work on the African-American.* New York: John Wiley.

Rocque, G. (1993, January). [Interview with elementary school teacher, Orleans Parish Public School System, New Orleans, LA.]

Rothman, D. J. (1971). *The discovery of the asylum: Social order and disorder in the new republic.* Boston: Little, Brown and Company.

Schermer, G. (1964-66). *Papers of George Schermer.* In (Vols. 5 & 6, Amistad Collection: Tulane University.

Seeman, M. (1983). Alienation motifs in contemporary theorizing: The hidden continuity of classic themes. *Social Psychological Quarterly, 46*(3), 171–184.

Spain, D. (1993). *Built to last: Public housing as an urban engendered space.* Paper presented to the annual meeting of the Urban Affairs Association, Indianapolis, IN.

Spear, A. H. (1967). *Black Chicago: The making of a Negro ghetto, 1890–1920.* Chicago: University of Chicago Press.

Stinchcombe, A. L. (1968). *Constructing social theories.* New York: Harcourt, Brace and World.

Teaford, J. C. (1990). *The rough road to renaissance: Urban revitalization in America, 1940–1985.* Baltimore, MD: Johns Hopkins University Press.

Thayer, R. (1978). *The evolution of housing policy in New Orleans, 1920–1978.* Unpublished manuscript, University of New Orleans, College of Urban and Public Affairs, New Orleans, LA.

Thayer, R., & Lorber, E. (1973). Urban problems of greater New Orleans — No. 2 at a conference entitled "Economic development of minority business enterprises in New Orleans." New Orleans, LA: The Institute.

Staff. (1924, September 19). *Times-Picayune,* pp. 1, 9.

Staff. (1924, September 17). *Times-Picayune,* p. 14.

Staff. (1924, September 10). *Times-Picayune,* p.7.

Staff. (1941, January 15). Prices for Land. *Times-Picayune,* p. 2.

Staff. (1956, April 17). *Times-Picayune.*

Staff. (1956, April 16). *Times-Picayune.*

Staff. (1956, April 18). *Times-Picayune.*

Staff. (1958, April 10). *Times-Picayune.*

Staff. (1958, May 29). *Times-Picayune.*

Staff. (1959, February 25). *Times-Picayune.*

Staff. (1959, February 21). A.P. Tureau fights Fischer. *Times-Picayune.*

Staff. (1960, September 16). *Times-Picayune.*

Staff. (1960, September 18). *Times-Picayune.*

Staff. (1960, August 28). *Times-Picayune.*

United States Bureau of the Census. (1940). Washington, DC: U.S. Government Printing Office.

United States Bureau of the Census. (1950). Washington, DC: U.S. Government Printing Office.

United States Bureau of the Census. (1990a). *Current Population Reports.* Washington, DC: U.S. Government Printing Office.

United States Bureau of the Census. (1990b). Households, families, marital status, and living arrangements. In *Current Population Reports.* Washington, DC: U.S. Government Printing Office.

United States Bureau of the Census. (1990c). *Statistical abstract of the United States: 1990 (110th ed.).* Washington, DC: U.S. Government Printing Office.

United States Housing Authority. (1939). *What the Housing Act can do for your city.* Washington, DC: U.S. Government Printing Office.

Wellborn, J. G., Connell, J. P., & Skinner, E. A. (1989). *Student perceptions of control questionnaire: A new measure of perceived control in children (school domain).* Rochester, NY: University of Rochester.

Wilson, W. J. (1987). *The truly disadvantaged: The inner city, the underclass and public policy.* Chicago: University of Chicago Press.

Wilson, W. J. (1992). *Race, class, and poverty in urban neighborhoods: A comparative perspective.* In Building strong communities: Strategies for urban change. Cleveland, OH.

Zunz, O. (1982). *The changing face of inequality: Urbanization, industrial development, and immigrants in Detroit, 1880–1929.* Chicago: University of Chicago Press.

CHAPTER 16

THE REPRODUCTION OF WHITE DOMINATION IN URBAN DESEGREGATION SCHOOLS:
THE POST-1970s

John H. Stanfield, II

It has been 13 years since my "Urban Public School Desegregation: The Reproduction of Normative White Domination" appeared in the pages of the *Journal of Negro Education* (Stanfield, 1982). The article was one of those impatient pieces characteristic of a young scholar too much in a hurry to make an important point. If I had known it would become a classic commentary on school desegregation, perhaps I would have paused a bit more. On the other hand, if I had paused to add more polish and diminish the fire, it may have become just another dull piece published in a distinguished journal forever lost in the vast forest of education literature.

It was written one blistering hot summer afternoon soon after I waved my hands in utter disgust and frustration in the university carrel where I was reviewing mountains of school desegregation studies. Rather than write the bland review of the literature as I had originally planned, I heard myself finally say, chuck it. I proceeded to write a critical sociology of knowledge essay on why I thought studies of urban school desegregation for the most part missed the picture as to why school desegregation in most places had done little more than reconfigure and reproduce normative

339

white domination in a nation-state in which race is a core attribute in the formation of human development, institutions, communities, and ecosystems. America, that is, as I would claim years later, is a race-centered nation-state in which race is a powerful socialization agency on routine everyday levels as well as on attitudinal and blatant attitudinal levels (Stanfield, 1991). It is absurd to assume, to extend the logic of this argument, that schools and educational processes can be divorced from the intricacies of race as an organizational and attitudinal agency (Stanfield, 1992). At most, as time has gone on in this society, race has changed its configuration rather than declined in significance.

While that last point — the changing configuration of race as socialization agency — was made prophetically in 1982 as the means of predicting what was in store for the future of urban school desegregation, certainly the events of the past two decades have born out what some may have viewed as a pessimistic gaze through a crystal ball. We are living through a crystallizing era which by the year is becoming increasingly dangerous. It began internationally with the racial and ethnic strife which began to sweep Eastern Europe, Africa, and Latin America as the Soviet Union crumbled and the Cold War came to a very eventful halt. The emergence of Japan as an economic power in the new world order has been greeted with disdain and fear as western powers witness the rapid decline of their eminence in a world in which no one is really in control any longer. It is becoming more and more apparent that the internationalization of high powered computer-based information access technology is creating new patterns of haves and have nots with stratification characteristics paralleling the past inequality divisions between western colonial powers and their non-western colonial subjects.

The changing globe with its accelerating episodes of massive ethnic and racial conflict, macro-economic shifts and hegemonic technological trends has been the context for a post-Cold War United States which is a debtor nation with declining fortunes as a used-to-be world power. The exportation of hundreds of American businesses and hundreds of thousands of American jobs abroad to cheaper labor regions and societies has joined with the growing impotency of American labor unions in undermining the prosperity of the white working class (Bluestone, 1982). Those economic factors plus others such as spiraling costs of health care, higher education, housing, and other consumer goods have done much to contribute to the deepening despair of the failing white middle class. This is especially the case among white males who as working- and middle-class members feel a vice-gripping squeeze between the rising fortunes of women and the growing politicization of people of color with their increasing numerical sizes and their high fertility.

The white frustration with their perceived loss of power and purpose has been seen in many disturbing ways over the past two decades (Newman, 1988). It was seen in the election of Ronald Reagan and then George Bush to the presidency of the United States. Reagan's overt racism toward African Americans and other people of color and Jews gave white supremacy groups a powerful go ahead signal resulting in the increase of public intolerance toward oppressed people. George Bush's use of racist tactics in his 1988 bid for the Presidency deepened the evolution of a norm of racial intolerance which has begun to deepen its roots and extend its branches in dominant public culture. The beating of Rodney King, the Clarence Thomas – Anita Hill controversy, the urban immigrant/race riots, and other recent high profile race-related incidents have all contributed to a time of dismal race relations. It will become more dismal as politicians and media continue to question the merits of affirmative action and other lingering remnants of a civil rights era long past and undoubtedly never to return.

These matters all come together to explain why it is that urban school desegregation continues to be as they say, a mixed bag. On the one hand, there are the more positive examples of school desegregation "working." There are school administrators, teachers, parents, and students who have worked in unison to create and maintain schools with positive multiethnic learning environments. There are desegregated school systems in which the achievement levels of African American students have no doubt increased over time.

On the other hand, there are cases of school desegregation efforts continuing to be ensnared with resistance efforts on the part of states, local governments, media, political parties, and orga-nized citizen groups. State and local officials in most areas have been reluctant to move beyond the symbolic in desegregating schools. The greatest symbolic desegregation efforts have been voluntary plans which in many cases simply have not worked or have placed the greatest burden on parents and students of color who are usually the ones in need of getting to the "better schools."

Rarely, in other words, do we find Euro-American parents volunteering to enroll their children in predominantly non-white schools. It has been found in some instances that receiving (in most cases suburban) school administrators and teachers of voluntary transfer students does little to incorporate the youngsters and their cultural experiences into the social fabric of the institutions.

The willingness of states and local governments to stay content with ineffectual voluntary school desegregation plans has much to do with the decline of federal intervention in state and local issues. The growing right of center inclinations of the three federal branches has had a chilling effect on efforts to force state and local governments to continue to implement school desegregation policies and civil rights policies in general (Bell, 1992). The major consequence of this will be increasing failure on the part of civil rights proponents to litigate successfully on behalf of parents and children of color in need of quality education. We observe in the 1990s a trend toward states refusing to hear cases or opposing cases which attempt to improve the quality of schooling for students of color through effective desegregation plans.

In 1995, for instance, the Connecticut Superior Court ruled that the isolation of poor students of color in Hartford schools was not the fault of the state ("Connecticut Wins School Bias Suit"). The implication of the ruling is that the state can keep its voluntary across town lines school desegregation plan intact as opposed to being instructed to desegregate. More than likely, the federal government will not attempt to overturn this state position since standing up and behind civil rights issues is not politically trendy in this day and age. We can expect the Connecticut case to be the opening of the door to rolling back efforts to do what is necessary to provide quality education for poor children of color.

The federal reluctance to support aggressively school desegregation issues in American cities has much to do with the triumph of Reaganism and Bushism in strategically placing federal court appointments and developing a public cultural environment in which speaking on behalf of the socially disinherited, especially black folks, is out of style. It has become the era of blaming African Americans for their societal difficulties and using them as scapegoats for the declining fortunes of Euro-Americans. The right wing political style has been buttressed by the shift of national political economic power from cities to suburbs, ex-urbs and international regions. It has become almost appropriate for politicians, Republicans and moderate Democrats (à la Republicans) to dismiss the relevance of cities since schools have become racialized symbols politicians manipulate to gain votes through advocating law and order to control unruly, drug-infested "ghetto residents." The recent national popularity of urban school administrators renowned for their stern control is a case in point to how much inner city schools have become cultural commodities created by media and politicians and consumed by publics in desperate fear of black people (especially black males).

The cultural commoditization of urban education has been one more reminder of how much the civil rights movements of 30-plus years ago barely dented the underlying normative racialism which is interwoven throughout the fabric of American life. Even though the movement certainly brought to the surface the moral atrocities of racism and managed to pressure politicians into passing civil rights laws and implementing civil rights policies, it did little to root out the deepest areas of normative racialism. It did not dismantle the segregated quarters of the private lives of Americans regardless of socially defined race (Bell, 1992; Blauner, 1989; Cruse, 1987). As much as attitudes about racial integrating in public spaces have liberalized over time, the same cannot be said regarding attitudes regarding who Americans choose to befriend, marry, worship with, adopt, and who they assume is a leader, smart and trustworthy. In those cases, when it comes to primary group issues and to power and privilege matters, most Americans continue to racialize their views. This is why the rate of inter-racial marriage (white-black), especially among the elite classes, still is so minute. It is why most Americans continue to have friends only within their racialized categories. It is why most Euro-Americans and African Americans continue to live in segregated communities. It is the reason why so many Euro-Americans continue to be surprised to see African Americans playing roles outside racialized stereotypes and why so many African Americans continue to be just as surprised. It is the reason why shop-keepers assume that African Americans have the propensity to shop-lift and why so many professors assume that African American students who write well and count well must be cheating. It is why most Americans assumed that at best Jesse Jackson was a black presidential candidate who could not possibly win since who besides African Americans could possibly vote for an African American for President of the United States.

The persistence of historical normative racialism is seen in how quickly and zealously the media and segments of the public are regarding dismantling affirmative action. The willingness on the part of journalists to distort the meaning of affirmative action through pretending that it means the promotion of the incompetent has done much to suggest how uncomfortable Euro-Americans are when it comes to African American social mobility and success. It has become too much to many Euro-Americans to see African Americans driving around in BMWs, attending the best schools, and living in good neighborhoods (Feagin, 1994). This is the way it has always been because the belief that African Americans do not deserve to have anything is very much part of the dominant mind set which keeps them under. In the extent to which African Americans have taken advantage of the perks of societal desegregation, they have become unbearable competitors to Euro-American power and imagery. Thus, African Americans, in the eyes of the national white press and public, need to be put back in their place.

The Bell Curve (Hernnstein & Murray, 1994) is the most recent example on the part of Euro-American media and politicians to put black folks back in their place. It is not the poor and needy the book's authors are attempting to attack as much as affluent African Americans who are simply becoming too competitive. It creates the impression that African Americans are not deserving of their mobility since, as the authors attempt to demonstrate, all African Americans are dumb and stupid.

The Bell Curve also brings to mind the dangerous ways in which class and racial issues are beginning to collide in this era. It is becoming more than apparent that the present racial backlash the book symbolizes is coming at a time in which the nation-state is in serious debt and its dominant middle and working classes are disintegrating (Newman, 1988). The major economic problem with urban schooling is that no one can pay the bill. Neighborhoods, municipal, state, and federal government are all doing poorly in most locations. It has not been uncommon to hear of urban school systems filing bankruptcy and/or being taken over by for-profit organizations.

The book rationalizes an excuse for those in power to cease finding costly solutions to urban education. This is done of course by the authors strongly suggesting that the problems African Americans have in achieving are bio-genetic and pathologically cultural. If that is indeed the case, so the logic goes, there is no need for school policymakers to squander scarce financial resources on such useless populations. This exercise in rationalization through the abuse of scientific logic, methodology, and interpretation sets well with an Euro-American working-class and middle-class public experiencing deep frustration regarding their declining quality of life. Instead of facing the music of a globalizing economy with a deeply financially troubled America as a used-to-be world power, it is more comforting to many Euro-Americans to blame their societal problems on minorities and immigrants who are getting more than what they deserve.

There are other patterns which have made school desegregation very much of a dysfunctional experience in many American urban and rural communities. Several of these patterns should be briefly pointed out. First, the desegregation of African American faculty and administrators in suburban and magnet urban schools continues to lag behind the desegregation of African American students in such schools. This continues the historical trend of African American administrators and teachers being displaced during the first phase of school desegregation processes. There are two consequences of the persistent scarcity of African American teachers and administrators in suburban-based desegregated schools. The first consequence is the social cap placed on the career and mobility of African American teachers and administrators in predominantly affluent white school districts.

The second consequence is the absence or extreme scarcity of identity and cultural role models for African American students and students in general. We are seeing the end result of this second consequence in the number of African American young people who may be attending high quality, desegregated schools, but who experience difficulty in understanding who they are and do not learn how to cope in a race-centered society. Many of these students may be well-heeled in many respects but they lack the sophisticated cultural learning African American children used to receive in segregated African American schools. Their naive approach to the world begins to become problematic as they enter college and/or the labor force and discover but not understand that no matter what their class background is, race becomes a barrier to their quality of life and mobility. This is why so many affluent

African American parents who moved to white suburbia are now so adamant about enrolling their children in historically black colleges. The experiences of these professionals with the crystallizing glass ceiling of the 1980s has sobered them enough to force them to re-assess the assimilationist orientations which they embraced and passed down to their children as first cohorts in the desegregation of schools, communities, and work-places in the post-1960s.

The issue of school desegregation has become increasingly convoluted with issues of economic class. Those African American students most likely to be in segregated urban schools are more than likely of low socioeconomic status. Those middle-class African Americans with means like their Euro-American class counterparts have managed to buy their way out of poorly financed inner city highly segregated schools through geographical mobility or through sending their children to private schools. Meanwhile, the private school option for poor African American children continues to decrease as inner city Catholic schools, long in the business of subsidizing the education of the impoverished, close their doors or move to the suburbs.

The class division between the educational opportunities of the African American middle and poor classes has been exacerbated by the popularity of the voucher option in many parts of the country. The voucher system, by giving parents the right to place their children wherever their resources allow, is a class biased policy since only middle-class parents have the resources to use programs to their advantage. The voucher system is a back-door way to assist middle class parents with children entrapped in low quality schools due to residence or school desegregation to flee from such institutions. Only African American middle-class parents and middle-class parents in general would have the transportation resources and access to information necessary to move their tradition to high quality schools elsewhere in cities and in suburbs.

The evolving tendency for school desegregation to be intimately linked to economic class matters is a subset of the changing economic histories and functions of cities (Bluestone 1982; Fusfeld & Bates 1984; Orfield 1993; Wilson 1987). The deindustrialization of American cities has accelerated over the course of the past two decades due to the migration of basic industries from cities to suburbs, rural areas, and poor non-European nation-states and regions. What has been left behind have been economic vacuums filled by informal labor markets and illicit drug trafficking. The absence of adequate job opportunities and the crumbling of community institutions from families to churches to businesses has created social environments quite counter to what is needed to encourage young people to do well in school, graduate, and to go on to better opportunities. In too many inner cities, schools have not only become quite segregated, but also places where there is not an interest on the part of administrators, teachers, and students of engaging in learning experiences. If anything, too many segregated schools have become prisons with wide open doors for those who are least likely to have the resources to do constructive things with their lives. Even though in their own cultural terms, the victims of indifferent urban segregated schools may be "happy and content," their significant degrees of satisfaction do not contradict the tragic realities of what must be done to be a success in a capitalistic society with rigid mobility rules. If they are not gaining the skills essential for upward mobility from language to math, then it makes no difference how much such students happily learn how to rap, dance, and recite the histories of great African civilizations. The fact of the matter is, they may never know what this nation-state and world has to offer those who not only maintain a healthy sense of ethnic identity but who learn how to master the system enough to become upwardly mobile into the most influential places in the American nation-state.

The dismal portrait sketched in this chapter is not meant to be a prophecy set in stone. The mixed results of urban school desegregation can become more effective. This can happen by community leaders in urban settings becoming more willing to establish citizen groups. Parents and their children as well as community people must begin to take matters into their own hands to hold legislators and media more accountable. It is important for community leaders to begin to come together and organize consumer boycotts and other protest movements against media and businesses that are financing the resistance to desegregation in their neighborhoods. Over and beyond, there is a need for local community leaders to form coalitions across ethnic lines with other people of color within communities and across the country to advocate the needs of young people in desegregated schools.

But before that happens, African Americans must become much more clear about what they want out of enrolling their children in desegregated schools. Is it desegregation (access to resources such as teachers and curriculum)? Is it assimilation (cultural co-optation), is it pluralism (understanding other cultures) or some combination? Just what is it we really want? These questions are important research and policy issues for future generations of scholars interested in what has remained the normative reproduction of white domination in urban public schools. They are important issues since the good intentions of the *Brown* decision have now been overwhelmed by historical and political shifts as well as changes in generations. Different times demand different questions and different solutions. In the midst of these changes we must decide what we want for our children and our future descendants in the midst of a society which will continue to pluralize. Otherwise, we will continue to fall to the whims of a nation-state that continues to turn its back on us, and in general, on the plight of the disinherited.

In writing this chapter, I wish I could have been more uplifting and otherwise positive. But, these are hard times which require hard, critical thinking. The liberal way of doing things simply has not worked for African Americans over the long haul and the same goes for those who prefer more radical or conservative perspectives. The 1990s have been a time in which all traditional ideologies about race relations and about African Americans in general have been discredited or viewed as too limited. We are in a desperate need to stop attending the church of our choice among the standard political camps and begin to search our minds and hearts for more realistic ways of dealing with issues such as urban school desegregation. That is why I so strongly suggest organized political action (Stanfield 1992). Until we re-group and advocate the needs of our children, African American survival is in danger. This is especially the case when it comes to the African American poor who are the most expendable in a society which prefers to ignore them or criminalize them in popular imagery. Unless we begin to do something for our children in schools, regardless of our social class, we will all be like the seeds in the Biblical parable which all went to the wayside.

If the recent rise of the Republican Party in Congress, the continued waffling of moderate Democrat Bill Clinton, and *The Bell Curve* have taught us anything, it is that we are all, regardless of class, in this together. Thus, regardless of the dominant public cultural rhetoric which so conveniently divides African Americans along class lines, as long as poor African American children continue to be denied the privilege of a decent education, the African American middle class will continue to experience mobility limitations since the powerful in this land see us as being from the same ship.

References

Bell, D. (1992). *Fares at the bottom of the well: The permanence of racism.* New York: Basic Books.

Blauner, B. (1989). *Black lives, white lives: Three decades of race relations in America.* Berkeley, CA: University of California Press.

Bluestone, B. (1982). *The deindustrialization of America.* New York: Basic Books.

Connecticut wins school bias suit. (1995, April 13). *The New York Times*, p. 1.11.

Cruse, H. (1987). *Plural but equal.* New York: William Morrow.

Feagin, J. R. (1994). *Living with racism: The black middle class experience.* Boston: Beacon Press.

Fusfeld, D. R., & Bates, T. (1984). *The political economy of the urban ghetto.* Carbondale, IL: Southern Illinois University Press.

Hernnstein, R. J., & Murray, C. (1994). *The bell curve.* New York: Free Press.

Newman, K. (1988). *Falling from grace: The experience of downward mobility in the American middle class.* New York: Free Press.

Orfield, G. (1993). *The growth of segregation in American schools.* Alexandria, VA: National School Boards Association, Council of Urban Boards of Education.

Stanfield, J. H., II. (1982). Urban public school desegregation: The reproduction of normative white dominance. *Journal of Negro Education, 51*, 90–100.

Stanfield, J. H., II. (1990). American businessmen and the ambivalent transformation of racially segregated public schools. *Phi Delta Kappan*, September, 63–67.

Stanfield, J. H., II. (1991). Racism in America and other race-centered societies. *The International Journal of Comparative Sociology, 32*, 243–260.

Stanfield, J. H., II. (1992). Ethnic pluralism and civic responsibility in post-Cold War America. *Journal of Negro Education, 61*, 287–300.
Wilson, W. J. (1987). *The truly disadvantaged.* Chicago: University of Chicago Press.

CHAPTER 17

MEDIA MEDIOCRITY:
A PERSPECTIVE ON HIGHER EDUCATION DESEGREGATION NEWS COVERAGE IN THE SECOND RECONSTRUCTION

J. Dale Thorn

In his book *The Fifties*, David Halberstam (1993) lauds the career of Frank McGee, the unlettered north Louisianian who found himself in Montgomery, Alabama, the cradle of the Civil Rights movement, in the mid-1950s. McGee performed so admirably in covering the movement's birth that he became one of NBCs first national correspondents, within a year of the Montgomery bus boycott settlement. It was a simpler time. McGee had grown up poor. In an age when top journalists were products of elite universities, Frank McGee had never gone to college. He finished a high school equivalency course while serving in the military. The more complex days of the Second Reconstruction could have profited from more Frank McGees.

In 1979, almost a quarter century after McGee's distinguished coverage, Benjamin Hooks lamented the news media's confusion and shortsightedness in covering the National Association for the

The author is indebted to the Louisiana State University Council on Research and the Freedom Forum Professor Publishing Program for grants that assisted in conducting the research for this article.

Advancement of Colored People (NAACP). Hooks, then executive director of the NAACP, urged the media to distinguish between his organization and the NAACP Legal Defense Fund (LDF). Observing in 1979 that the NAACP and the LDF had separated more than two decades earlier, in 1957, Hooks noted that the distinction between the two had eluded the grasp even of "knowledgeable newsmen" (Hooks, 1979, pp. 187-88).

In the tidal wave of NAACP news coverage in 1994, centering on the firing of Benjamin Chavis, the media exhibited a similar mediocrity. News organizations gave massive attention to the sexual and financial misconduct allegations against Mr. Chavis and to his links with Minister Louis Farrakhan. But ironically, in a year when Mr. Chavis forged for the NAACP a far more assertive role on the higher education desegregation front, the news media and their willingness to settle for mediocrity stood in the way of coverage. That they missed the larger story — the NAACP's tortuous travail on one of the burning legal, social, and political issues of our time — suggests anew that the media are quick to cover the failures of well-known personalities, but slow to engage the public on complex stories that beg for historical context.

The NAACP's higher profile in the college and university desegregation arena occurred in the spring of 1994. Shortly before the beginning of the end for Chavis and just before the 1994 retrial of *U.S. v. Fordice* (1992), Chavis and NAACP President Rupert Richardson led a march in Jackson, Mississippi, of some 15,000 African American students from around the nation to protest Mississippi's proposed merger of Mississippi Valley State University with Delta State University (Mercer, 1994).

It was an event that should have raised a red flag in the minds of journalists. For the NAACP is not just any organization. It is the one organization that had kept its eyes on the prize of desegregated education for all Americans. Locally and nationally the NAACP stood as a beacon to those who looked to *Brown v. Board of Education* (1954) as requiring desegregation throughout education, not just race-neutral policies. When NAFEO (the National Association for Equal Opportunity in Higher Education), an organization of more than 100 Presidents of Historically Black Colleges and Universities (HBCUs), pleaded in the early 1970s that *Brown* did not apply to public colleges and universities, the

NAACP stood steadfast in support of *Brown's* reach. Indeed, its position signaled the first rift between major civil rights organizations on the central meaning of *Brown* (Haynes, 1978). To the NAACP and the LDF *Brown* meant that the HBCUs must be desegregated as well. The NAACP's 1994 position before the retrial of the Mississippi case represented not just a change, but an about-face. The media's unquestioning reporting, whether based on a lack of knowledge or a willingness to look the other way when African Americans opt for segregation, missed an opportunity to illustrate desegregation's complexity when the issue reaches the postsecondary education threshold. (See Chapter Two for further discussion of this rift between the NAACP and NAFEO.)

The pertinent history was available in the NAACP's own files. Its 1973 resolution on university desegregation committed the organization to the "total integration of all tax-supported institutions serving the public." It called on branches in the 19 affected states to engage in dismantling the dual higher education systems, with the dual, proximate institutions to be "merged equitably." Desegregation should ensure protection of African American students, faculty, and administrators in the process, the resolution added. And for the remaining HBCUs, the NAACP urged equitable appropriations so that they could "effectively compete with predominantly white colleges." Unequivocal at the outset, the resolution declared that state-supported HBCUs "were established by public officials to perpetuate segregation . . ." (NAACP, 1993, pp. 22–23).

The NAACP's local chapters fell in line. "The only way black equity in education can be achieved," said Emmitt Douglas, then Louisiana NAACP chapter president, "is through a unitary, integrated system where black students have the same advantages and opportunities as whites" (Edgerton, 1974, p. 36). Yet there were more than a few discordant notes as African American leaders contemplated mergers. And they had ample reason, given what had happened to predominantly African American schools and communities in desegregation at the K–12 level. Schools had been closed, communities had been disrupted, and African American educators had generally sacrificed their top leadership positions in the South's elementary and secondary schools. Richard Turnley, Jr., an African American member of the Louisiana Legislature, summed up the mainstream middle-class African

American opposition to the NAACP's position: "We want a separate but equal situation. We accept that" (Edgerton, 1974, p. 36).

In the face of such opposition, the NAACP lowered its profile. The cleavage within the African American community went largely unreported. Neither the national press nor the local press distinguished themselves. By the early 1990s NAACP officials had concluded that campus mergers constituted one segregation remedy, but not necessarily the only remedy (Richardson, 1990). The shift had been glacial, but it, too, went unreported in the news media. It was a case of media mediocrity magnified. In defense of their performance, they could claim that no one could be sure just what the law required, for the U.S. Supreme Court had yet to accept a case that would define the extent of desegregation remedies in the higher education setting.

The Supreme Court Decision

In June 1992, in the case of *U.S. v. Fordice* (1992), emanating from Mississippi, the Supreme Court finally ruled. In *Fordice* the court first held that the lower courts had failed to place the burden of proof where it belonged. (See Chapters Two, Fourteen, and Fifteen for further discussion of this case.) Instead of placing the burden on plaintiffs to prove that segregation exists, as the district court had, the Supreme Court overturned the district court and Fifth Circuit Court of Appeals decisions. The Supreme Court sent the case back to the district court with a singular admonition: The 19 formerly de jure segregated states (and only those with that history) bear the burden of proving either that there are no remaining vestiges of the de jure era or that any remaining vestiges of state-imposed segregation are educationally sound and impractical to overcome:

> If the State perpetuates policies and practices traceable to its prior system that continue to have segregative effects — whether by influencing student enrollment decisions or by fostering segregation in other facets of the university system — and such policies are without sound educational justification and can be practicably eliminated, the State has not satisfied its burden of proving that it has dismantled its prior system. Such policies run afoul of the Equal Protection Clause, even though the State has abolished the legal requirement that

whites and blacks be educated separately and has established racially neutral policies not animated by a discriminatory purpose. (*U.S. v. Fordice*, 1992)

In short, the Supreme Court placed the HBCUs and their white counterparts at risk in the 19 states, enunciating a requirement that the states justify the dual situations or eliminate them. Moreover, in that same ruling, the Supreme Court all but invited the state of Mississippi to close some campuses, a fact not well reported. Addressing dual higher education systems for the first time since *Brown*, the Supreme Court agreed with the district court in Oxford that the existence of eight senior universities in Mississippi "instead of some lesser number was undoubtedly occasioned by state laws forbidding the mingling of the races." "And as the District Court recognized," the Supreme Court added, "continuing to maintain all eight universities in Mississippi is wasteful and irrational" (*U.S. v. Fordice*, 1992).

After the Court's 8–1 ruling, with only Justice Scalia dissenting, civil rights leaders hailed the decision as a victory. The NAACP was in the vanguard, quoting approvingly from parts of the decision it liked. Justice Sandra Day O'Connor's concurring opinion had cited Mississippi's "long history of discrimination." Justice Clarence Thomas's concurring opinion had concluded that *Fordice* "portends neither the destruction of historically black colleges nor the severing of those institutions from their distinctive histories and traditions" (NAACP Legal Department, 1992, pp. 2–3). What the NAACP and the media failed to say, however, was that *Fordice* was more a procedural victory than one of substance. For by sending the case back to the district court in Mississippi with a clear signal to close some institutions, no one could be assured of victory, a fact that was focused upon by neither the media nor the NAACP.

The NAACP acknowledged, however, that "significant issues remain as to the future existence of all eight of [Mississippi's] colleges and universities and whether maintenance of each is compatible with constitutional standards" (NAACP Legal Department, 1992, p. 3). The organization could counter only with an assertion: "The maintenance of historically Black institutions with all of their academic diversity and established traditions and programs . . . is both educationally sound and constitutionally permissible" (NAACP Legal Department, 1992, p. 3).

The NAACP's ambivalence found its latest expression in a 1994 resolution marking the 40th anniversary of *Brown*. The organization said it would pursue higher education desegregation "together with the enhancement of historically Black colleges and universities . . ." (NAACP, 1994). To many, the NAACP's formula sounded remarkably like the judicially rejected Louisiana formula of the 1980s: Plow new money and programs into the African American campuses but require no desegregation. The Reagan administration's education secretary, Terrel Bell, once summed up that administration's attitude in similar fashion: "I don't want to make the Black colleges whiter; I just want to make them better" (Arceneaux, 1981). More than a decade later, the Clinton administration's education department, announcing its intention to use *Fordice* as a yardstick in the 19 states, nonetheless acknowledged that it would "strictly scrutinize" any state proposal to close or merge HBCUs. African American leaders in higher education praised the department's statement (Jaschik, 1994).

Paul Greenberg, the astute Arkansas editorialist, writing of what he called The New Segregationism of the 1980s, explained that what made it different from the old was that the justification of separate but equal was "practiced on behalf of the minority, not against it" (1992, p. 170). Greenberg observed of that era:

> No [segregationist] ever defended predominantly white schools more effectively than predominantly black colleges are defended today. Ralph Bunche's old warning would surely be denounced as racist on many a black campus now: We cannot prepare people to function in an integrated society by educating them in segregated institutions. (Greenberg, 1992, p. 170)

While the NAACP was not endorsing segregation, its position came quite close to accepting segregation. Forty years after *Brown*, and 21 years after adopting its resolution in favor of mergers, the NAACP was opposing a merger in Mississippi that would eviscerate an HBCU, one with fewer than a dozen white students.

Shortly before the 1994 retrial in Mississippi, the Jackson, Mississippi *Clarion–Ledger* sent reporters around the state to capture the mood of Mississippians as the trial neared. The newspaper reported a general state of confusion among Mississippians about why the trial was necessary (Wagster, 1994). A convenience sample of the *Clarion–Ledger* before and during the two-month trial reveals that the newspaper told readers that the case was based on inequalities in Mississippi's higher education system, informed them that the Supreme Court had overruled the judge's previous decision against the African American plaintiffs, and observed that the case was being watched by 18 other states. (The 19 states confronting the legal mandate to desegregate higher education range from the Deep South to Texas, Arkansas, and Oklahoma in the Southwest, on to the Atlantic Coast states in the Southeast, and then to the Border States, as well as Ohio, Pennsylvania, and Delaware.)

What the *Clarion–Ledger* did not report, according to the convenience sample, was that the case was based on Mississippi's and the other 18 states' history of state-imposed segregation and the fact that it was that history that placed the 19 states in a legal posture different from their sister states. In covering such trials the media could no doubt contribute to public understanding by including in their daily reports a simple explanation. The 19 states have one mark in common: They once had laws on the books requiring that African American and white college students attend racially separate public colleges.

The Un-Covered Expert

That one elementary omission in the trial's coverage, while important, was only the most basic. A full day of testimony would go unreported. A livid Elias Blake, president of the Benjamin Mays Center in Washington, DC, and the African American plaintiffs' chief expert witness, was dumbfounded at the omission of his testimony. "The reporter from the leading newspaper in the state did not report a single word of my testimony," said Blake. "The *Clarion–Ledger* has consistently been biased against the private plaintiffs" (Blake, 1994). Asked to respond, the reporter explained that he had left the courtroom during Blake's testimony to work on a piece for the Sunday paper (Kanengiser, 1994). Blake concluded that the *Clarion–Ledger* did little to resolve the confusion reigning in Mississippi. "The media don't understand the case," he declared. "In the eyes of the media, we can't get out from under the desire for separate education" (Blake, 1994).

What the media failed to understand, he said, is the way the "whole system . . . works to keep blacks out" (Blake, 1994). Racial balance was not the principal issue, "but who gets in [college] and who gets prepared to get in" (Blake, 1994). Mississippi's community colleges should be parties to the lawsuit, he contended, for they represented a denial of access to four-year colleges. The higher the percentage enrolled in two-year institutions, the lower the number of baccalaureate graduates for both African Americans and whites, he testified. For African Americans who start at community colleges, only 9% complete the baccalaureate degree. Worse still, Blake testified, 70% of the 1994 Mississippi Valley State graduates would lack the test scores necessary to gain admission to the proposed Delta Valley State University, the would-be product of the Delta State-Valley merger.

Interviews with opposing attorneys over four days of the trial found, conversely, that the plaintiffs' attorneys were positive and the state's attorneys negative in their assessment of the *Clarion–Ledger*'s coverage. Plaintiffs' attorney Alvin Chambliss said he could not criticize the local or regional media. He thought they were fair. What puzzled him was the absence of national coverage. "I've really been surprised and disappointed with media coverage on the national level," Chambliss said. "This is the most important issue for black people in America today. I really don't think the seriousness of this has caught on nationally. People don't understand, and the populace drives the media" (Chambliss, 1994). State counsel William Goodman of Jackson found the Associated Press and the Memphis *Commercial Appeal* fair and balanced. Goodman complained that the *Clarion–Ledger*'s approach to covering the trial was "to print the most extreme statement. If there's nothing sensational in the courtroom, go out and interview people." When President James Lyons of Jackson State University testified that Jackson State was not interested in taking over the University of Mississippi Medical Center (a plaintiffs' proposal to further desegregation), the *Clarion–Ledger* ignored it, Goodman charged. "If Lyons had testified he wanted it, it would have been headlines" (Goodman, 1994). To complaints from both Goodman and Blake, *Clarion–Ledger* reporter Andy Kanengiser (1994) observed that the newspaper is not a paper of record. The two sides did not realize, he said, the difficulty of covering the trial daily while preparing enterprise pieces for the weekend editions.

Although a number of major newspapers and two networks published or broadcast stories on the Mississippi case in advance of the trial, the only newspaper in court on a daily basis was the *Clarion–Ledger.* The Memphis *Commercial Appeal* covered the trial occasionally. The Associated Press was the only national medium there daily, using a local stringer for the most part. The highly regarded *Chronicle of Higher Education* chose not to cover the trial after the first week. Neither did it publish a report at the trial's conclusion.

Califano and North Carolina

When Joseph A. Califano Jr., became secretary of Health, Education, and Welfare in 1977, he found the issues surrounding the legal mandate to desegregate higher education "as complex and subtle as any I faced" (Califano, 1981, p. 244).

The HBCUs that had come into being after the Civil War provided opportunity to African Americans who, "both discriminated against and badly instructed, couldn't get into even the least demanding White schools," Califano observed in his book *Governing America* (Califano, 1981, p. 244). He ultimately failed in his legal effort to deny federal funds to the University of North Carolina (UNC), when it refused to go along with his approach of transferring academic programs from historically white campuses to HBCUs to encourage racial balance (Consent Decree, 1981).

North Carolina's battle with Califano and the bureaucracy gained the widest coverage of any state. Viewed as prestigious in academe and progressive on race, North Carolina was expected to be a leader in dismantling the dual higher education system. And Califano knew that if he could break North Carolina, the other Southern states would fall in line. But the coverage of the Califano-North Carolina confrontation in the early 1980s represented some of the most egregious, knee-jerk conclusions and reportage yet seen. The media committed a number of errors, and those errors colored much of the reporting in the aftermath.

The coverage and commentary of even the prestige press in the early years of these cases was marked by inaccuracy and distortion, particularly in *The New York Times*. A *Times* editorial in the early 1980s ("North Carolina's College Deal," 1981), alleging that UNC had violated desegregation court orders on two occasions, was reprinted in the Raleigh *News and Observer*. Its appearance prompted U.S. District Judge Franklin T. Dupree, in a rare judicial notice of media coverage, to observe in a decision handed down in his North Carolina courtroom, that the editorial was "simply erroneous" (Consent Decree, 1981).

Apparently feeding off the printed press, the highly regarded CBS *Sunday Morning* program — hosted then by UNC graduate Charles Kuralt — aired a 10-minute segment on the UNC case just two months later, with footage of Governor George Wallace standing in the schoolhouse door at the University of Alabama in the early 1960s, a gross stereotype. The coverage sparked a furor in North Carolina, and with egg on its face, *Sunday Morning* gave UNC President William Friday a five-minute on-the-air response (Link, 1995). *Sunday Morning*, like much of the media, had failed to tell its audience that these cases are far more complex than the stand-in-the-door flouting of 1960s court orders. Ultimately these cases are about both racial balance and the removal of the vestiges — the remnants — of state-imposed segregation. It is a context essential to understanding the higher education cases.

Besides the gaffes and stereotypes of the media elites, American journalism, print and broadcast, provided a dearth of relatively simple, interpretive, what-it-means reporting on the higher education desegregation arena. PBSs otherwise commendable *Eyes on the Prize II* failed even to mention higher education desegregation in the South. And in its all-too-brief coverage of the *Regents of the University of California v. Bakke* (1978) decision, *The Prize II* failed to point out that *Bakke* emanated from a state with no history of state-imposed (de jure) segregation in higher education. Thus, the U.S. Supreme Court decision in *Bakke*, holding that race may be a plus in the file but not the sole factor in college admissions, does not apply to admissions decisions in the 19 states that once excluded students by law on the basis of race. In those states, race may be the sole, decisive factor. The nation needs to understand these distinctions.

Perhaps the most egregious example of media mediocrity occurred in June 1993, when the Atlanta newspapers failed to cover a hearing on the Alabama higher education desegregation case at the Eleventh Circuit Court of Appeals in Atlanta, the first occasion on which an appellate court was called upon to interpret *Fordice*. Though it occurred in Atlanta, the Alabama case hearing failed to receive coverage in either the local editions of the Atlanta papers or their Alabama editions. The *Montgomery Advertiser* gave the hearing cursory coverage, running a wire service story that focused on courtroom rhetoric but failed to explain the far-reaching issues. Additionally, Montgomery is home to the lead plaintiff, state Rep. John F. Knight, Jr., coordinator of communications and public affairs at Alabama State University. The Montgomery newspaper's performance was reminiscent of the civil rights movement's robust days, when the Montgomery newspapers, rather than cover a local story themselves, ran a wire service story of the march from Selma to Montgomery (Halberstam, 1993, p. 559). Consistent with the inadequate coverage of the Atlanta hearing, not one mainstream medium, including those in Alabama, bothered to profile Mr. Knight in the 14 years the case had been pending. Nor on the day after the hearing did the media bother to cover Mr. Knight's reaction to the appellate hearing.

The Alabama case, *Knight v. Alabama* (1991) raised some issues not yet posed in other states. And it raised them in a more compelling way than any case in the 1990s, notwithstanding the greater amount of ink and video given the Mississippi case. *Knight* looked beyond numbers. The case raised for the first time the quality of the racial climate on campuses and what would be taught on the historically white campuses to make them more attractive to African Americans. *Knight* came to the Eleventh Circuit after a nine-month District Court trial that led to a 300-page opinion (*Knight v. Alabama*, 1991). Besides seeking $125 million in new buildings for Alabama State and Alabama A&M, the state's historically black campuses, Knight and the other plaintiffs asked that the black institutions share "flagship" status with Auburn University and the University of Alabama. Additionally, they sought African American studies programs on the historically white campuses.

The district court had denied every major claim the Alabama plaintiffs put forth, except for the conclusion that the state had failed to eliminate the vestiges of segregation and that the two HBCUs failed to share in state funding, both capital and operating, in an equitable manner. Instead of $125 million for new buildings, however, the district court awarded $30 million. By prevailing on the liability question in the District Court, the conclusion that remnants of segregation remained in the state's higher education system, Knight was awarded $1.9 million in attorney fees. But he wanted more than money.

The Eleventh Circuit obliged, at least in remanding a number of critical issues for further consideration by the district court. The higher court ordered the district court to re-examine the plaintiffs' inferior missions' claims on behalf of the two HBCUs, along with Auburn's exclusive hold on state land-grant funds, and notably, the plaintiffs' desire for more African American studies programs on white campuses. The district court should balance the plaintiffs' proposed curriculum remedy, the Eleventh Circuit said, with the faculties' First Amendment academic freedom interest in determining what will be taught. In each case, the court said, the District Court must weigh the remaining vestiges of segregation, in accordance with *Fordice*: not on the basis of whether the state institutions have adopted and enforced race-neutral policies, but on the scales of whether the remaining vestiges of segregation have continuing segregative effects. If the segregative effects linger, the courts must determine whether those effects "can be remedied in a manner that is practicable and educationally sound" (*Knight v. Alabama*, 1994). The new trial was pending in spring 1995.

Today at 49, Knight is a member of the Alabama Legislature. What he really wants now, he acknowledges, is to see Alabama State University (and its sister institution, Alabama A&M) win flagship status, gaining the treatment accorded Auburn and the University of Alabama. To those who suggest that what he's asking for is just another version of separate but equal, Knight points out that, with a 99% African American enrollment, Alabama State could hardly be more separate (Knight, 1993). It is a point of view that the news media fail to impart.

An Absence of Penetrating Reporting

Incisive, penetrating reporting would be especially helpful, from a regional perspective, in treating the substance and outcome of the court cases. Almost none of the reporting emanating either from the Southern press or from the prestige press beyond the South has compared or contrasted the different means used to desegregate universities. Journalists now have enough data to draw some comparisons. In 1977 a federal court in Tennessee in *Geier v. Blanton* (1977) ordered a merger, the most radical remedy, of Tennessee State University (TSU) and the University of Tennessee-Nashville, with the former named as the surviving institution (*Geier v. Blanton*, 1977). After considerable white flight, the court in 1984 set as a 1993 goal for Tennessee State a 50–50 racial mix, applied to students, faculty, and staff (*Geier v. Alexander*, 1984). Latest enrollment data indicate that white students make up about 32% of TSUs enrollment, despite the merger and a heavy infusion of capital improvements on campus.

With five public HBCUs, North Carolina has the largest number in the nation. Unlike Tennessee, North Carolina refused to merge institutions, close them, or transfer academic programs between historically white campuses and HBCUs. Today at Fayetteville State, one of North Carolina's HBCUs, whites account for a third of the enrollment. How did it happen? UNC officials say it was a case of a dynamic chancellor who embarked on genuine recruitment efforts, along with a sophisticated network of high school counselors and generous financial aid packages for deserving students (Simms, 1994).

That kind of remedy is clearly more subjective, more personality-oriented, more dependent upon good faith than the remedy employed in the Tennessee case. But North Carolina's remedy, emanating from a consent decree after the state sued the federal government to prevent the termination of federal funds, has achieved about the same result at Fayetteville State as the Tennessee remedy did at Tennessee State. The North Carolina result is one that has been achieved at far less cost and with far greater consensus.

Louisiana's attempt to follow North Carolina's legal path failed. When Louisiana signed a consent decree (*U.S. v. Louisiana*, 1981), it called for the infusion of capital improvements and new degree programs at Southern University and Grambling State. When the decree expired six years later, a federal court concluded that the state's HBCUs were more segregated than before the decree (*U.S. v. Louisiana*, 1989). In effect, efforts to enhance the HBCUs had made them more attractive to their traditional clientele: African American students. The attentive public never sees these kinds of state-to-state comparisons in the news media. Thus the casual reader, listener, or viewer comes away from learning about a new court decision with the idea that there may be some magic-bullet approach to stimulate higher education desegregation when, in fact, different approaches over time may work in different ways in different places. Each state's media become absorbed in that state's case, and rarely does any significant coverage cross state lines. The wire service coverage of one state's case seldom is picked up beyond neighboring states facing the same issues. News editors frequently fail to see the significance of one to the other. A more comprehensive look at what is happening in the states, rather than a glance at each in isolation, would yield greater understanding.

In November 1994, the district court in Louisiana backed away from an earlier threat to merge institutions and boards, approving a new 10–year settlement that called for another $122 million in new academic programs, structures, and affirmative action strategies (*U.S. v. Louisiana*, 1994). The settlement, perhaps anticipating a landmark land-grant decision in the Alabama case, remained silent on equity in land-grant funding at Southern University and LSU, leaving that for further negotiations or trial. (See Chapter 14 for a further discussion of the Louisiana case.) Dissenting voices were few, but one was the voice of Rupert Richardson, NAACP national president as well as president of the Louisiana NAACP chapter. Richardson, who had long been on record in favor of merging Louisiana's four governing boards, contended that the settlement would only enhance Louisiana's "separate but equal" approach to higher education (Dyer, 1994, pp. A1, A4). But the failure of the NAACP and the Legal Defense Fund to challenge the settlement in court suggested another acceptance of segregation, provided the HBCUs remained intact.

A leading Louisiana editorial page was less charitable, though resigned. *The Advocate* of Baton Rouge contended that the settlement was not about desegregation, higher education, or the efficient use of tax dollars, but rather about money, turf, and obstacles to an effective statewide community college system. Still, said *The Advocate*, "The positives might even outweigh the negatives" ("Education pact about $$$, turf," 1994, p. B6). Rationalizing the difference between the settlement of 1981 and 1994, Education Secretary Sally Clausen said, "This focuses on graduate programs; the other focused on undergraduates. This focuses on quality; the other focused on quotas" (McConnaughey, 1994, pp. 1–6). If the two settlements had anything in common, it was that they preserved Louisiana's four HBCUs, the predominantly black Southern University governing board, and the three predominantly white governing boards. Neither the decree of 1981 nor the settlement of 1994 required desegregation.

In the days of the robust civil rights movement, the news media were called upon to provide coverage of what amounted to an appeal for simple justice. Justice at that time entailed tearing down the walls of legal, state-imposed segregation in every facet of public life. In those days the media performed admirably. In the face of official efforts to silence the press, *New York Times v. Sullivan* (1964), a case that emanated from the civil rights era in Alabama and gave the media greater protection against libel suits in criticizing public officials' public performance, was but one testament to the national media's courage and tenacity in exposing state-sponsored segregation. Today there are no states making concerted efforts to impede media coverage of the Second Reconstruction. Unlike the 1950s and 1960s, justice is less simple, more complex. It would only add to the recent record of media mediocrity in news coverage if, at a time when the media are free to expand coverage, they decided that the story was not adequately inviting.

The failure of the news media to provide the audience the larger context gave the NAACP a free ride on the higher education desegregation front. The media, occupied with the more apparent story of scandal at the NAACP, failed on the larger public policy front to hold accountable the organization that is synonymous with desegregation. News organizations would have served the nation better if they had reported the organization's long, and apparently anguished, travail as it departed from its earlier moorings.

As for trial coverage, it is clear from the Mississippi experience of the summer of 1994 and the Atlanta experience of the summer of 1993 that newspapers are missing an opportunity in the one venue where cameras and recorders cannot go: the federal courts. The printed press must accept much of the responsibility for the public's confusion about the higher education desegregation cases. Whether they fail to inquire into the NAACP's past, ignore an appellate hearing in a case from a neighboring state, fail to tell the full story of what's happening in the courtroom, engage in reporting that abets broadcasters' stereotypes, fail to interview or profile African American plaintiffs, or ignore the legal thread common to the 19 affected states, the newspapers are settling for mediocrity. We should not be surprised if the reader finds the current level of racial discourse less than illuminating.

In the fullness of time, historians will no doubt find that the mediocre news coverage of the era fails to provide leads and insights to the important primary documents of university desegregation controversies. One question that raises its head immediately is, Where are the Frank McGees of today? The easy answer is that the federal courtroom allows no visual coverage, that there could be no Frank McGee today. The tougher questions demand far more. Those questions would begin with the observation that not one print reporter has gained a national reputation for coverage of the major racial controversy that pervades the Second Reconstruction in its twilight.

As the national debate on affirmative action begins, there is a void of news coverage observing that the HBCUs, born of affirmative action on behalf of African Americans, are now being measured by their ability to engage in affirmative action on behalf of white students. The distinguished historian C. Vann Woodward would no doubt observe, the advent of affirmative action on behalf of white students is but another irony to the burden of southern history.

References

Arceneaux, W., Louisiana Commissioner of Higher Education. (1981). [Interview by author, September 27, Baton Rouge, LA.]

Blake, E., President of Benjamin Mays Center, Washington, DC. (1994). [Interview by author, June 2, Oxford, MS.]

Califano, J. A., Jr. (1981). *Governing America: An insider's report from the White House and the Cabinet.* New York: Simon and Schuster.

Chambliss, A., private plaintiffs' counsel, *U.S. v. Fordice.* (1994). [Interview by author, June 2, Oxford, MS.]

Dyer, S. (1994, November 15). Higher ed settlement ok'd. *The Advocate*, pp. A1, A4.

Edgerton, J. (1974, December/January). *Adams v. Richardson*: Can separate be equal? *Change*, 36.

Education pact about $$$, turf. (1994, November 9). *The Advocate*, p. B6.

Goodman, W., state counsel, *U.S. v. Fordice.* (1994). [Interview by author, June 2, Oxford, MS.]

Greenberg, P. (1992). *Entirely personal.* Jackson, MS: University Press of Mississippi.

Halberstam, D. (1993). *The fifties.* New York: Villard Books.

Haynes, L. L., III (Ed.). *A critical examination of the Adams case: A source book.*

Hooks, B. L. (1979, June/July). Historical revisionism. *The Crisis*, pp. 187–188.

Jaschik, S. (1994, February 9). Education Department to use 1992 Supreme Court case in judging formerly segregated state systems. *The Chronicle of Higher Education*, p. A36.

Kanengiser, A., *Clarion Ledger* reporter. (1994). [Interview by author, June 2, Oxford, MS.]

Knight, J. F., Jr., communications and public affairs coordinator, Alabama State University. (1993). [Interview by author, July 1, Montgomery, AL.]

Link, W. (1995). William Friday: Power, purpose and American higher education. Chapel Hill, NC: University of North Carolina Press.

McConnaughey, J. (1994, November 15). Officials pleased with settlement. *The Daily Reveille*, pp. 1, 6.

Mercer, J. (1994, May 11). Marching to save black colleges. *The Chronicle of Higher Education*, p. A28.

National Association for the Advancement of Colored People. (1994). 40th anniversary of *Brown v. Board of Education, 1994*. Baltimore, MD: Author.

National Association for the Advancement of Colored People, Education Department. (1993). *Resolutions on education, 1970–1993*. Baltimore, MD: Author.

National Association for the Advancement of Colored People, Legal Department. (1992). Statement on *United States v. Fordice*. Baltimore, MD: Author.

North Carolina's College Deal. (1981, July 11). *The New York Times*, p. A22.

Richardson, R. (1990, spring semester). Remarks to opinion journalism class. Louisiana State University, Baton Rouge, LA.

Simms, N., vice president, University of North Carolina System. (1994). [Interview by author (telephone), May 10.]

Wagster, E. (1994, May 9). *Ayers*: Is there an answer? *Clarion–Ledger*, p. A1.

Table of Legal Cases

Consent Decree, North Carolina v. Department of Education, No. 79–217–CIV–5, slip op. (E.D. N.C., 1981).

Brown v. Board of Education, 347 U.S. 483 (1954).

Geier v. Alexander, No. 5077, slip op. (M.D. Tenn. 1984).

Geier v. Blanton, 427 F. Supp. 644 (M.D. Tenn. 1977) *affirmed sub nom.*

Geier v. University of Tennessee, 597 F.2d 1056 (6th Cir. 1979), *cert. denied*, 444 U.S. 886 (1979).

Knight v. Alabama 787 F.Supp. 1030 (N.D. Ala. 1991).

Knight v. Alabama, No. 92-6160, slip op. (11th Cir. 1994).

New York Times v. Sullivan, (376 U.S. 254) (1964).

Regent of the University of California v. Bakke, 438 U.S. 265, 98
   S.Ct. 2733 (1978).
U.S. v. Fordice, 60 U.S.L.W. 4773 (1992).
U.S. v. Louisiana, 80–3300–A, slip op. (E.D. La. 1981).
U.S. v. Louisiana, 80–3300–A, slip op. (E.D. La. 1989).
U.S. v. Louisiana, 80–3300–A, slip op. (E.D. La. 1994).

CHAPTER 18

A LOOK TO THE FUTURE:
INTRODUCTION TO SECTION IV

Kofi Lomotey and Charles Teddlie

Section IV, A Look to the Future, continues two of the themes noted in the book's Introduction and in other section introductions:

1. The general tone of pessimism is again conveyed in the four chapters in this section. The authors of all four chapters conclude that the current state of affairs regarding school desegregation is not what proponents of the *Brown* decision had envisioned.

2. Three of the chapters offer specific suggestions for improvement in elementary-secondary education (Chapters Twenty-one and Twenty-two) and in higher education (Chapter Twenty). Such suggestions are offered in ten of the chapters in this volume.

In Chapter Nineteen, Cheryl Brown Henderson (the daughter of Rev. Oliver Brown who was listed as the plaintiff in the *Brown v. Board of Education* suit) and Shariba Rivers share their thoughts regarding the legacy of *Brown* as it relates to community and familial relationships. They begin by noting that although the *Brown* decision is one of the most significant events in the history of the U.S., it is also one of the most misunderstood. They further explain that examinations of this case seldom deal with the complex constitutional issues or the history that underscores the

369

sacrifice and self-determination present in the African American community.

Henderson and Rivers add that although *Brown* sparked a period of social responsibility, equity, and justice that had not been witnessed since the end of the Civil War, it also presented and continues to present challenges in the form of policy and implementation as neighborhoods divide along racial lines and public resources dwindle. They also address other issues such as educational experts spending little time looking for solutions and an enormous amount of time identifying scapegoats, the ambivalence involved in the telling of the *Brown* story, and the unanticipated legacy of *Brown* which represents the insidious nature of what the school desegregation pioneers were up against then and what continues today.

In Chapter Twenty, Jerold Waltman discusses the future of public HBCUs. He suggests that although public HBCUs are a vital national treasure, their futures will remain clouded as long as they remain under the current system of governance. He further argues that advocates of equal educational opportunity are seeking incompatible goals because, on the one hand, they propose more desegregation at both historically white and historically black institutions. Yet, at the same time, they proclaim that it is important that HBCUs remain African American in character. In conclusion, Waltman recommends the establishment of a governing board under the jurisdiction of the federal government as the best approach to building a successful future for public HBCUs.

In Chapter Twenty-one, Kofi Lomotey and Richard Fossey discuss the ineffectiveness of school desegregation in the U.S. According to these authors, the educational experience of many African American students is deteriorating, particularly in the nation's inner city school districts and in the rural South. For instance, they note that 40 years after *Brown,* not only are African Americans and Hispanics more likely to drop out of school than white students, they are also more likely to be placed in special education. In addition, suspension and expulsion rates are higher for African American students than for white students (far higher for African American males).

Moreover, Lomotey and Fossey indicate that if *Brown* had improved educational opportunities for African Americans, we would expect to see improvements in African American economic status. However, a recent U.S. Census Bureau report reveals that more black families, not less, have been sinking below the poverty line in recent years. They add that although courts have played a crucial role in desegregating schools (getting whites and African American children into the same school), they have failed to prepare teachers who can effectively respond to children's cultural differences. To create a more effective educational system, they recommend (a) introducing culturally equitable pedagogy in the classroom, (b) providing effective, competent and compassionate teachers and school leaders, (c) reorganizing schools into safe and nurturing environments, and (d) honestly addressing the issues of inequality in society and in schools.

Drawing, in part, upon the work of Harold Cruse and others, Shujaa and Johnson, in Chapter Twenty-two, offer an interesting discussion of two conflicting — yet complementary — thrusts within the African American community: integration and nationalism. They refer to these thrusts as social order restricted thinking and social order transcendent thinking, respectively. To highlight the distinction, they offer analyses of school desegregation in the U.S. and the development of the Council of Independent Black Institutions, as examples of integrationist and nationalist thinking respectively.

An underlying theme in Chapter Twenty-two is that the social order restricted thinking (of which school desegregation is an example) limits the practitioner to working within the system and does not speak to the need to alter existing power relationships. (See Chapter Sixteen, where Stanfield makes this point also.) The social order transcendent thinking, on the other hand, addresses changing power relationships and issues of self-determination.

CHAPTER 19

The Legacy of *Brown* 40 Years Later

Cheryl Brown Henderson and Shariba Rivers

The U.S. Supreme Court decision of May 17, 1954 *Oliver L. Brown et al. vs. The Board of Education of Topeka* (KS), is one of the most significant events in the history of this country. Yet, it is one of the most misunderstood. Examinations of this case seldom deal with the complex constitutional issues or the history that underscores the sacrifiee and self-determination present in the African American community. Even fewer accounts of the *Brown* decision provide information about the specifics of the Topeka case such as the local NAACP leadership, attorneys, the 13 plaintiffs representing their 20 children and those unknown individuals whose lives were changed by these events. History books rarely mention that the *Brown* decision was a joining of five cases from Delaware, Kansas, South Carolina, Virginia, and the District of Columbia. The thoughts shared in this writing regarding the legacy of *Brown* come from the vantage point of community and familial relationships. The *Brown* decision is named for an African American man who in 1950 was a 32-year-old parent. Although his participation was almost coincidental, the fact remains that it is his name that is attached to what is one of the most pivotal events in U.S. history.

373

Let us begin by clarifying any misnomer that the *Brown* case was dinner time conversation in the Brown home. It was not. Reverend Oliver L. Brown died in 1961, ten years after this suit was filed, seven years after the U.S. Supreme Court's decision and before the media sophistication of court TV. He only participated in one televised interview before his death. His wife and daughters had to become students of *Brown* just like the rest of the country in order to learn and understand what took place. Having pored over historic documents, photos, and published works, the importance of the *Brown* decision is now clearly etched in their minds.

Brown is important for four very basic reasons:

1. It was the beginning of the end of legally sanctioned racial segregation.

2. It overturned laws permitting segregated public schools in Kansas and 20 other states.

3. It overturned a previous U.S. Supreme Court decision of 1896, *Plessy vs. Ferguson.* The *Plessy* decision gave us the infamous doctrine of "separate but equal."

4. It defended the sovereign power of the people of the United States to protect their natural rights from arbitrary restrictions and limits imposed by state and local governments. These rights are recognized in the Declaration of Independence and guaranteed by the Constitution of the United States.

The legacy of the *Brown* decision can be viewed from both the anticipated and the unanticipated perspectives. The unanticipated legacy has clearly been the most disturbing. Elaboration on this point will come later in this chapter. The anticipated legacy, as we see it, is one of: (a) Beginnings; (b) Challenges; (c) Responses; and, (d) Myths.

Beginnings

Brown began a series of legal victories in the courts and eventually the U.S. Congress. This decision ushered in an avalanche of cases and legislation affecting African Americans and other disenfranchised groups in society. This was a critical juncture because it began a period of social responsibility, equity, and justice that this country had not witnessed since the end of the Civil War. With regard to people of African descent the last national acts of conscience came in the form of the 13th, 14th, and

15th amendments to the U.S. Constitution and the Civil Rights Act of 1875.

The Supreme Court's ruling in *Brown* had an impact on: equity in public transportation (1956); the Civil Rights Act (1964); the Voting Rights Act (1965); Title IX (1972); Section 504 of the Rehabilitation Act (1973); the Age Discrimination Act (1975); and the Civil Rights Restoration Act (1984), which did not become law until 1988. This litany, although not inclusive, represents a period of opportunity rarely seen before *Brown*.

Challenges

The move to end racial segregation in public schools presented and continues to present challenges in the form of policy and implementation. After the *Brown* decision, many well-meaning, law-abiding school districts moved to end segregated schools immediately. From 1954 to 1958, they numbered nearly 800. From 1958 through 1960, less than 100 joined their ranks. The reason for this slowdown was confusion on the part of decision makers relative to just how serious the federal government was. Where was the executive order or the congressional mandate to end this practice?

In Kansas, the school boards began to adopt muddled policies in order to deal with desegregation, some even before the *Brown* decision. One example surfaced in the form of a letter from the superintendent of schools in Topeka, Kansas. The year was 1953 and the letter was intended for newly hired (three years or less) African American teachers. Its content, in short, explained that if the U.S. Supreme Court should end racially segregated public schools, there would not be enough teaching positions for African American teachers due to the certainty that whites did not want them to teach their children.

Up until 1954, Kansas and numerous other states permitted variations on the theme of segregated public schools. Cities with a population of 15,000 or more were only required to segregate public schools at the elementary level. These cities were considered to be "first class cities" and therefore were not obligated to segregate public schools at the secondary or high school level. However, smaller cities were not protected by this state law.

Immediately following the *Brown* decision in May of 1954, public school officials went into action. As a result of the decision, officials felt that one of their major concerns would be an over-abundance of African American teachers. In order to deal with this concern, the officials simply did not renew some of the teachers' contracts. The remaining African American educators were placed into previously segregated schools where the administrators would first phone the parents of white students seeking permission for their children to be assigned to African American teachers.

Policy and implementation continue to present challenges as neighborhoods divide along racial lines and public resources dwindle. For example, there have been municipal decisions to create low-income housing which usually ends up being predominantly African American and which usually means that the closest school in the district will consist of a majority of African American students from low-income families. These school districts receive less attention than the predominantly white districts and consequently receive less resources, funding, and quality teachers. The least experienced teachers are being placed in these schools and are facing problems they never knew existed. These teachers start feeling overwhelmed and drop out of the system either physically or mentally, waiting for a better opportunity. Because they are suffering, the children suffer.

In addition to the problems of the division of housing along racial lines, there has been a decrease in the number of African American teachers because of lack of motivation to pursue the teaching profession as well as the lack of resources in order to offer salaries comparable to those in other professions. The field of educational administration has seriously low numbers of African Americans because of the low numbers of teachers aspiring to such positions. Those who are in the field consistently report that they are placed in predominantly African American districts replete with organizational problems, fiscal mismanagement, financial burdens, and lack of resources (Moffett, 1981; Wilkerson, 1985).

Responses
The *Brown* decision created a storm of responses in the way society in general and some whites in particular reacted. Those responses brought us the infamous "Southern Manifesto," or "the document of non-compliance." This manifesto was orchestrated by some U.S. congressional representatives from Southern states. The existence of such formal dissent gave power to local officials

in Southern communities to stand against what they saw as unwelcome government interference.

Without the Southern Manifesto it may not have been so simple for the governor of Arkansas, Orval Faubus, to close public schools for a year. This same support led public officials in Prince Edwards County, Virginia to close public schools for four years. The same sentiment was present when the governor of Alabama, George Wallace, took his stand in the school house door literally and figuratively to block the doors of segregated public schools. In the 1970s, that misplaced sense of right resulted in angry mobs of whites in Boston, Massachusetts meeting school buses filled with African American children, to halt the desegregation of public schools.

The country is still in a response mode. As a society, we spend little time looking for solutions and an enormous amount of time identifying scapegoats. In addressing the educational needs of this country, "experts" continually make the children (the victims) the root and cause of the problems. Statements such as "the children are too violent" or "they don't respect authority" are made to divert the country's attention away from the real issues. Instead of addressing the conditions and the circumstances that have brought this country, and these children, to such a violent and immoral point, these "experts" continue to suggest that the problem is the children and not the system.

These aspects of the *Brown* legacy come from the peculiar position of the United States Supreme Court and its limited enforcement authority. In some ways the struggle to interpret and implement the *Brown* decision may be attributed to the Court's early attempt to give direction to its intent, that is, "with all deliberate speed." How much difference would it have made had the court not offered this statement as an approach to the desegregation of the nation's public schools.

As the Brown family has come to understand *Brown v. Board of Education*, it is easy to see that the legacy is much more profound for African Americans. It is profound because African Americans, living in this country, were expected to fight its wars and economically support it without benefit of the basic right to enjoy the fruits of their labor. They repeatedly watched their children's spirits broken as they were coming of age in America. Let it not be forgotten that historically it was against the law for people of African descent to obtain an education — unlike any other racial or ethnic group in this country.

Brown is also profound because although many people think of it as the culmination of a legal battle waged for more than a century, it has proven to be more of a midpoint in school desegregation and race relations. It took African Americans 105 years just to get as far as *Brown*. The first lawsuit challenging the system of racially segregated public education was in 1849, the *Roberts* case in Boston, Massachusetts. This is a battle that followed people of African descent leaving the South after the Civil War, many of whom chose Kansas to start a new life. Kansas was considered a "promised land" of sorts because it did not allow the enslavement of people and offered the hope of education, land, and liberty.

Even in this land of promise, African Americans found it necessary to take up the banner of desegregated schooling to achieve equal opportunity. In Kansas, 12 lawsuits were filed regarding school desegregation. These cases run from 1881 with the *Tinnon* Case in Ottawa, Kansas to 1949 with the *Webb* Case in Merriam, Kansas. The twelfth case in Kansas was *Brown*, filed in 1951.

Myths

The legacy for the Brown family has been filled with ambivalence in the matter of the telling of the *Brown* story. The children and widow of Oliver Brown have been left a legacy not of their own making. Jack Greenberg (1994) points out in his book, *Crusaders in the Courts*, that because the U.S. Supreme Court chose the *Brown* case to head the school cases, it gave immortality to a family who had little to do with this struggle.

The legacy that the Brown family shoulders is a story created by a lazy and myopic press. Their creation was sold to the public and taken as fact, so much so that it has been a tale repeatedly printed in articles and textbooks since the decision. The press created a story of a young girl who wanted to attend her neighborhood school, but because she was African American she was forced to attend another school far from her home. Her father was so angered over the issue of segregated schools and the question of their legality that he sued the local school board. This fabrication hides the real issues and keeps us from the truth. The story negates the psychological impact that segregation had on both African Americans and white Americans. It relegates to the back burner those who had the vision, persistence, and knowledge to see this legal challenge to its conclusion.

The story also conveniently fails to detail all of the other efforts toward desegregation prior to this case. Examine the facts closely and then look at the story the press would prefer we believe. First remember that the pursuit of legal recourse to end segregated public schools began in 1849 with the *Roberts* case. Secondly, remember that the U.S. Supreme Court's decision in *Brown* combined similar cases from Delaware, South Carolina, Virginia, and the District of Columbia. These cases were part of a sweeping strategy devised by the NAACP (LDEF–Legal Defense and Education Fund). Thirdly, remember that African Americans in Kansas initiated eleven school cases prior to *Brown*.

The events in Topeka, Kansas that led to *Brown* are as follows. In the late 1940s the local chapter of the NAACP had considered what should be done regarding the situation with its public schools. The chapter president McKinley Burnett attempted a reasoned approach by asking for time on the agenda of local school board meetings. His efforts resulted in the equivalent of a filibuster. The meetings would extend beyond a tolerable hour, adjourning because of the time without getting to Mr. Burnett's agenda item. It was obvious that another tactic was needed. This led to talk of a court case. At that point Mr. Burnett, together with local NAACP legal counsel Elisha Scott, sons Charles and John Scott, associate Charles Bledsoe, and chapter secretary Lucinda Todd, laid out a framework for what would become the *Brown* case. Their plan would be simple once they rallied the support of local parents needed as plaintiffs.

The summer of 1950 saw the gathering of 14 families who stepped forward to become litigants. By that fall, 13 families remained, including the family of Oliver Brown. They were asked to note enrollment dates, locate the segregated white school closest to their homes and, together with another adult as a witness, attempt to enroll their children. Once denied the right to enroll their children, they were to share the details of that experience with NAACP legal counsel. This information would provide the basis for a class action suit against the Topeka Board of Education.

When the case was filed in Federal District Court in February of 1951, a peculiar event occurred. Oliver Brown was designated as the lead plaintiff although he had little else to do with their plan other than to participate. As we have reviewed this development, one conclusion has surfaced — sexism may have played a role in the naming of this historic case. Among the list of plaintiffs, Oliver Brown was the only man. The Brown family had been told over the years that the Brown name was selected to head the list because of alphabetical placement. Yet, one of the female plaintiffs' name was Darlene Brown which means that if the alphabetical placement story were true, she should have been the one chosen to head the list. It seems that the NAACP chose Oliver Brown over Darlene Brown because they felt that the case would have more power behind it with a male as its lead plaintiff.

Although Reverend Brown's role, in truth, was minimal, the legacy of *Brown* is one that the Brown family has grown to bear proudly. The responsibility they have assumed is that of telling the *Brown* story as it happened. The reality is much more profound than the press creation. It does make one wonder how many other events in our history were concocted and then repeated as fact.

Finally, let the country not forget that it was Charles Hamilton Houston that laid the groundwork and litigated early cases to end segregated public schools and universities. His brilliant work resulted in unparalleled success in the courts for the NAACP Legal Defense and Education Fund (LDEF). He mentored Thurgood Marshall and a host of other young civil rights attorneys.

Unanticipated Legacy

The unanticipated legacy of *Brown* represents the insidious nature of what the school desegregation pioneers were up against and what still continues today. That legacy has been:

1. School closings because of white flight, a proliferation of white private schools, and magnet schools.

2. The majority of African American students remaining in segregated schools that are lacking money, resources and attention.

3. The scarcity of African American teachers.

4. The *Regents of the University of California v. Bakke* (1978) case.

5. Busing as a tool for desegregation that turned into a tool for segregation.

However, the most insidious legacy of all is the continuous effort to somehow show that African Americans are not capable of intellectual achievement. Throughout history white Americans have tried to negate the African American's intellectual capacity through all kinds of "scientific" and psychological research. Books such as *The Bell Curve* (Herrnstein & Murray, 1994) are ever-present and ever ready with scientific "facts" to prove some sort of intellectual inferiority. Our children and our society have been labeled "at risk" and "culturally deprived" in order to be placed in sub-categories to other people and other cultures. As our national demographics become more diverse, racially divisive attitudes such as these struggle to hold on.

For the Brown family, the unanticipated legacy has been one of ongoing litigation against the Topeka Board of Education in what is known as *Brown III* (1992). The fact of the matter is that in the fall of 1979, Topeka Public Schools had instituted a policy called "open enrollment" that would permit students to freely transfer from school to school. In response to this policy, a group of young African American attorneys convened a series of town meetings with African American parents and educators. The purpose of these meetings was to explain the potential harm of such a policy if left unchallenged.

As the school year progressed, their decision was to call into question the district's policy by petitioning the federal court to re-open the original *Brown* case in Topeka. In order to have a lawsuit, they needed plaintiffs. They believed that this group of parents should include someone associated with the original *Brown* case, so who better than a child of the lead plaintiff, Oliver Brown. As a result, they assembled a group of eight families whose names were to be submitted as litigants, including the Brown family. Once filed, those parents lending their names to this case were not called on to participate in any other action. The case did not go to trial until 1987. It was not concluded until 1993 when a Federal Appeals Court found that Topeka Public Schools did have vestiges of past school segregation and ordered remedy (*Brown III*). The remedy selected was to close older schools within the district and build three new magnet schools.

Conclusion

The Brown Foundation was established to commemorate and document the stories of the true history-makers whose memories are not recounted in books. The Foundation continues to engage in activities to affect the myth that is *Brown*. The foundation has produced a traveling exhibit and teaching materials for classroom use. In 1992 after two years of work with the U.S. Congress and the Department of the Interior, the Foundation established a National Park to interpret the history of the *Brown* decision and school desegregation. On October 26, 1992, President George Bush signed the *Brown vs. Board of Education National Historic Site Act of 1992*. This legislation marked the official designation of this new national park.

The site of this national park is located in Topeka, Kansas at the site of one of the previously segregated schools for African American children — Monroe Elementary School. Plans are underway for its opening in 1998.

References

Greenberg, J. (1994). *Crusaders in the courts: How a dedicated band of lawyers fought for the civil rights revolution.* New York: Basic Books.

Herrnstein, R. J., & Murray, C. (1994). *The bell curve: Intelligence and class structure in American life.* New York: Free Press.

Moffett, T. D. (1981). A study of the upward mobility of blacks to top-level administrative positions in pubic school systems in the South. *Dissertation Abstracts International. 42,* 1413A.

Wilkerson, G. (1985). Black school administrators in the Los Angeles Unified School District: Personal perspectives and current considerations. *Dissertation Abstracts International. 47,* 2414A.

Table of Legal Cases

Brown v. Board of Education, 347 U.S. 483, 74 S.Ct. 686, 98 L.Ed 873 (1954).

Brown v. Board of Education, 349 U.S. 294, 75 S.Ct. 53, 99 L.Ed. 1083 (1955).

Board of Education of Topeka, Shawnee County of Kansas, v. Oliver Brown, et al., 89–1681 U.S. 978, 112 S.Ct. 1657, 118 L.Ed. 2d 381 (1992).

Plessy v. Ferguson, 163 U.S. 537, 16 S.Ct. 1138, 41 L.Ed. 356 (1896).

Regents of the University of California v. Bakke, 429 U.S. 953, 97 S.Ct. 373, 50 L.Ed. 2d 321.

Webb et al. v. School District No. 90, Johnson County, et al., 37427, 167 Kan. 395, 206 P.2d 1066 (1949).

CHAPTER 20

EXPLORING THE FUTURE OF BLACK PUBLIC COLLEGES: A PROPOSAL TO CREATE A NATIONAL SYSTEM

Jerold Waltman

Historically black public colleges and universities have an ambivalent legacy in the struggle to bring full educational opportunities to African Americans, and the heritage of that legacy creates acute dilemmas for educational policy makers as well as federal judges today. On the one hand, they were founded by people who obviously had no interest whatever in providing quality education for African Americans. Quite the contrary, in fact — their real interest was denying equal educational opportunities. On the other hand, these very institutions have proved to be invaluable to generations of African Americans. They have opened the doors of higher education to more African Americans than any other type of institution; they have offered a nurturing environment for many students; for many years, they provided the only enclave available for many African American scholars and

A briefer version of the ideas discussed here appeared in the Chronicles of Higher Education, July 6, 1994. I would like to thank Mr. Ronald Farris for sharing his extensive newspaper clipping file with me.

teachers. Consequently, most of them possess strong institutional identities and loyal supporters.

This dual legacy is evident as one surveys the history of desegregation cases in the federal courts. In the early years, in order to open up historically white universities to qualified black applicants, the NAACP argued forcefully that the education available in historically black colleges (HBCUs) was decidedly inferior to that available elsewhere.   Many black educators doubted the wisdom of this strategy, however, even at the time. Jean Preer (1982) has aptly labeled this the saga of *Lawyers v. Educators.* (See Chapter Two for a further discussion of this issue.)

In the area of public elementary and secondary schools, the Supreme Court repeatedly ordered that the states must operate unitary school systems, with no school being identifiably white or black (*Alexander v. Holmes County Board of Education*, 1969). If this mandate is applied to higher education, it necessarily means the end of public HBCUs. as we know them. They will either be closed or become merely state colleges, proud perhaps of their heritage but in their contemporary operation indistinguishable from other public institutions of similar size and scope.   The alternative is for them to remain identifiably African American in curriculum, environment, faculty, and student body. If they are successful in this endeavor, though, is that a formula for resegregation?

This dilemma is closely tied to the issue of the best way to integrate American life. Is the appropriate route for African Americans as individuals to become a part of the mainstream institutions of American society? Or, would it be preferable for African Americans to build their own institutions and integrate as a group? In truth, both strategies are needed, but how does each of the HBCUs fit into that debate? An even more basic question is who should make that decision?

It is my belief that the nation's public HBCUs are a vital national treasure, and that now is the time to think more broadly about their future than we have in the past. In my view, that future is clouded so long as they remain under the current system of governance. Policy makers and commentators alike have unnecessarily narrowed the choices they examined in this regard, and it is time to think in broader terms. It is time to free these institutions from the shackles of the past by restructuring the arrangements for their governance.

My position is that these institutions need to be removed from the umbrella of the state governing boards which have overseen them in the past and placed under the jurisdiction of a public entity which is solely concerned with them. Realistically, this can only be accomplished under the aegis of the federal government. In this chapter I will explain why I think this step is needed, argue that the only analogy is the self-examination Catholic colleges had to go through a few decades ago, and sketch out the details of my proposal.

The Underlying Framework

There are a number of factors that must be kept in mind whenever the future of public HBCUs is being discussed. The first salient point is that they should have never been built in the first place. Public colleges and universities in every state should have catered to students of all races and backgrounds from the moment their doors opened. Likewise, faculty and staff should have been recruited on merit alone. The University of Alabama or the University of Mississippi, for example, should have been the pride of all the citizens of those states, not just the Caucasian citizens.

To say that, of course, is to start an infinite historical regression: there should have been no segregation; there should have been no civil war; there should have been no slavery. At this point in time, however, none of those facts can be changed. HBCUs exist, and even if the Universities of Alabama and Mississippi become what they should have been all along, that would not mean that HBCUs should be shuttered up or made museums in the same way that dual water fountains should be torn down or made into memorials.

Second, without question, public HBCUs have always been treated as second- or third-class institutions. They were at the back of every educational bus the state drove, particularly the budgetary bus. Corners were cut in construction, as is evident to any casual visitor to most of the campuses even today; maintenance was woefully inadequate; salaries were abysmally low; libraries were severely under-stocked.

Working conditions were often nearly feudal. The administrators viewed their main task as keeping the flow of dollars coming to their campuses, meager though the totals were. To antagonize legislators or local white elites spelled serious trouble. Many ran their colleges therefore with an iron hand, employing "safe" faculty and keeping only docile staff members. The last thing an HBCU administrator needed was a faculty member who made waves. Additionally, of course, state officials, and sadly, even national institutions, were uninterested in the internal operation of these institutions.

But as important as the budgetary inadequacies was the open neglect and disdain with which the states treated these institutions. Not only were HBCUs budgetary stepchildren given the crumbs, they were constantly reminded that they were not really part of the family. When I worked in the financial office at Grambling College in the mid-1960s, for example, the state's statistical reports invariably listed the predominantly white institutions in alphabetical order, and merely appended Southern University and Grambling College onto the end. That gesture alone spoke volumes about where these institutions stood in the eyes of state officials. Similar symbolic slaps were a continual fact of life for HBCUs throughout the South.

Nevertheless, and the third factor to be kept in mind, despite the enormous handicaps under which they labored, public HBCUs were invaluable to the African American community. Although seriously underfinanced and relegated to the periphery of American higher education, they stood as beacons of opportunity, as centers of culture, as symbols of community solidarity through their sponsorship of athletic teams, literary competitions and so forth. They provided, too, an isolated pyramid of opportunity for African American scholars and administrators.

In short, they nurtured several generations of African Americans through the dark days of segregation and overt racism. For thousands upon thousands of African Americans they provided the only hope of acquiring a college education. Consequently, they have given the country most of its African American intellectual leaders, as well as the great bulk of its African American college graduates. What they accomplished is truly remarkable. To let them wither away would therefore be a major tragedy for all Americans, not only African Americans. (See Chapter Eleven for a further discussion of the importance of HBCUs.)

Fourth, given the history of governmental sanctioned racism in the South and the states' past neglect of the black institutions, a lingering and justifiable suspicion exists among African Americans that racism guides today's decision making. Of course, the old days are thankfully gone. Southern state governments have undergone an important metamorphosis (Black & Black, 1987). Black legislators, administrators, and policy makers are everywhere; the right to vote is secure (even if the drawing of electoral boundaries is contested); legal barriers to desegregation have disappeared. Nonetheless, the stigma of the past remains. Southern governmental institutions, including the various boards that operate systems of higher education, are still predominantly white, and there is still a certain degree of continuity with the past. It has proved more difficult than anyone imagined to expunge the ghost of racism and the suspicion of racism. The conditioning of the past is so strong that even if racism does not play a part in a decision, doubt always exist. This serves to poison the atmosphere, making rational discussion all but impossible.

Finally, while racism was and is deeper and more profound in the South than elsewhere, it also was and is a national phenomenon. The education of African American students is, therefore, not an issue that should be confined to the states with public HBCUs. Instead, it is a matter of national concern.

Although misguided decisions in Southern and border states (plus Pennsylvania and Ohio) led to the establishment of separate public colleges for African Americans, rectifying those decisions should not be something for which current citizens of those states are alone responsible. Contemporary residents of Alabama are no more heirs of those who built these colleges than the contemporary residents of Oregon.

To be sure, it was state governments in Alabama and elsewhere that erected the public HBCUs. However, to say that the government of Alabama must now stand fully responsible for correcting that mistake is to adopt a perverted view of federalism and intergenerational responsibility. It is to believe, regarding the former, that racism and its legacy are purely a regional matter, a proposition which can easily be demonstrated to be false. As for the latter, it is to believe that the sins of the fathers are to be visited only on those who now occupy the same ground as they did. Exorcizing racism from this country and overcoming its crippling legacy is something to which all Americans need to be dedicated.

To the extent that the future of HBCUs is bound up with that, they are the responsibility of the country as a whole.

The Inadequacies of Current Governance Structures

If we accept these propositions, it is doubtful that the boards of higher education in the South can ever craft acceptable plans for the future of HBCUs. The practical and ethical problems are simply overwhelming.

For instance, consider admissions standards. Should they be uniform at all of a state's public institutions? If so, that would likely undermine the special role that some HBCUs have played in meeting the needs of educationally disadvantaged students. If the standards are set rather high, the disadvantaged will not be able to attend any college in the system; if they are set rather low, it means every institution is catering to the disadvantaged. If, though, institutions develop different admissions criteria, it leads to a two-tiered system, a system in which the HBCUs inevitably will fall into the second tier.

What is the ideal relationship between the desegregation plans for a state's historically white institutions and its public HBCUs? The more aggressively formerly white institutions recruit African American students and faculty, for example, the harder it is for HBCUs to recruit students and faculty. The more scholarships and other inducements the historically white colleges offer African American students to enroll on their campuses, the fewer African American students there are for the HBCUs. The competition for talented African American youth — in academics, in athletics, in music, and so forth — has been intense for some time. This applies more generally as well. A recent proposal by the University of Southern Mississippi, for example, to offer an intensive summer remedial program for disadvantaged students, with an eye toward their admission to the university, was attacked by spokesmen for HBCUs as a raid on their clientele.

What should be done about institutions that are close to each other? Southern University is located in the same city as Louisiana State University; Grambling State University is less than five miles from Louisiana Tech University; Mississippi Valley State University and Delta State University are only forty miles apart; Texas Southern University is quite close to the University of Houston; Alabama State University shares Montgomery with Auburn University; Alabama A & M University and the University of Alabama at Huntsville are in the same city. Should these institutions be merged to avoid duplication, as the University of Tennessee at Nashville and Tennessee State University were? If so, how should that be done? The results of the Nashville experience have been mixed. (See Harrison, 1992 and Chapter Ten for further discussion of this merger.) If plans fall short of outright merger, should joint programs be encouraged?

On another front, should massive amounts of money be spent for the expansion and upgrading of HBCUs to make them "equal" in every aspect to the formerly all-white system? Should, for instance, every state have a major university created from its public HBCUs? Most of the states in which HBCUs are located, ironically, are the ones least able to afford large-scale expenditures on higher education. Many of them, in fact, already have more higher education than they can realistically support. Moreover, even if resources are poured into the HBCUs by the states, what is the goal? If the result is that more African American students choose to attend them instead of the historically white colleges, has resegregation occurred?

Should white students be encouraged to select HBCUs? The easiest way to accomplish this is to establish or move high demand programs to the HBCUs. The architecture school at Florida A & M University is often cited as an example of the successful building of an desegregated program at an HBCU. Conceivably, other professional programs could be erected at HBCUs with a similar result (although Louisiana's experience has not been encouraging). But if more white students are attracted, particularly to the regular baccalaureate programs, can a college maintain its identity as a black college? Will it inevitably become indistinguishable from other public colleges? If so, what is the point of struggling to keep it open in the first place?

Should the primary focus be on the needs of African American students or the needs of the HBCUs? These are by no means identical. Do African American students who elect to attend historically white institutions, for whatever reason, benefit more from efforts to upgrade HBCUs or from efforts to increase the quality of education available at their own institutions?

In short, advocates of equal educational opportunity are caught on the horns of an inescapable dilemma, as illustrated by the plaintiff's meanderings in the interminable *Ayers v. Fordice* (1992) case involving the higher education system in Mississippi.

On the one hand, they have argued for more desegregation at both historically white and historically black institutions. At the same time, they proclaim that it is important that HBCUs remain African American in character. Obviously, these are incompatible goals. For example, they concurred in a proposal by the Department of Justice to transfer the operation of the Universities Center in Jackson and the University of Mississippi Medical Center (also in Jackson) to Jackson State University. But a student leader at Mississippi Valley State University voiced the following sentiment: "If the courts say we have to have integration, that means an end to traditional black schools. It's not what I want. . . I want to go to a black school . . . The blacker the college, the sweeter the knowledge" (Grimm, 1991). (See Chapters Two and Ten for further discussion of the Mississippi case.)

Given these complexities, it is small wonder that state boards of higher education feel overwhelmed. Even if state officials act with the best of intentions, though, and honestly try to work through all these difficulties, their proposals will always have an aura of illegitimacy about them. No matter which direction they choose to take on any of the issues noted above, they can be charged with being racially biased, whether they are or not. Feelings about the segregated past, and, unfortunately, some current tensions (such as those that arose recently over the use of the Confederate flag in Georgia, Alabama, and Mississippi) are simply too strong. As historian David Sansing says, "Blacks in Mississippi have no tradition of trust. They aren't going to trust the so-called white leaders, and who could blame them?" (Historian, 1992)

The Transformation of Catholic Colleges after World War II

Thus, we need an entirely new approach, one that will sweep away the legacy of state-sponsored racism and allow HBCUs to find their niche in the higher education mosaic. The closest analogy to the situation facing HBCUs today is that of Roman Catholic colleges a few decades ago.

Before World War II Catholic colleges had a relatively clear role and a natural, built-in constituency. Catholic students naturally gravitated to such colleges, and found in them a distinctively Catholic education. According to Andrew Greeley (1969), Catholic colleges and universities were traditionally "part of the comprehensive ghetto" (p. 79).

However, in the years following the Second World War, as Catholics entered more decidedly into the U.S. mainstream and as opportunities in public higher education expanded (with the building of public commuter campuses in many urban areas, for example), the automatic bond between Catholics and their colleges dissolved. In response, Catholic institutions had to go through a period of self-examination, and delineate new missions. In 1969, Father Greeley wrote, "Catholic higher education . . . is . . . definitively departing from its original position within the walls of the immigrant ghetto, attempting to become part of the broader American higher educational enterprise" (p. 19).

Some chose to move closer to the secular model, emphasizing research, broadening the curriculum, and recruiting non-Catholic faculty and students (Power, 1972). Boston College, Fordham, and Notre Dame are but a few examples. Others chose to emphasize strongly their Catholic character, or some particular aspect of Catholicism. Aquinas College in Michigan with its widely known commitment to a traditional liberal arts core, or St. John's University of Minnesota with its Benedictine orientation, are but two schools that fall into this category. Still others developed or strengthened professional schools (Marquette and Georgetown), while many of those in urban centers created programs to meet the needs of inner city populations (DePaul). Most Catholic colleges succeeded in making the transition and survived to contribute to the diversity that characterizes American higher education.

The analogy is not perfect, of course. Catholic colleges are private, and more importantly, Catholics were never forced by law to attend them. Nevertheless, the parallels between the two situations are close enough to be suggestive. In both cases, colleges connected to a group that is becoming — individually and collectively — more desegregated into American society have had to grapple with the implications of that desegregation. Catholic colleges did not outlive their function as Catholics fully melted into American life. They did, however, have to change in order to retain their vitality.

From the same perspective, some HBCUs could find an important niche by specializing in some aspect of the African American experience, such as literature, history, or art. Others might find an important institutional mission in specialized professional education in business, health care, engineering, or other fields in which the numbers of African Americans are low.

Still others might wish to devote their energies to general bacca-laureate education for educationally disadvantaged African American students. Then, some might move closer to mainline colleges and universities, and, while not shedding their African American heritage, work to attract students and faculty members of all races.

There are, in sum, all kinds of patterns and models available, and there need not be one mold. What direction a particular institution could most profitably take would undoubtedly depend on its size, its location, its proximity to other institutions, its present strengths, and so forth.

Creating a New Governance Structure for Public HBCUs

Whatever role various HBCUs adopt, these decisions can best be discussed, dissected, debated, adopted, implemented, and modified by people whose first and only priority is the fate of these institutions. The contemporary governance structures are inadequate to the task, both because they are rooted in the policies of the past and because they have other institutions to govern. A governing body needs to be established that deals only with black colleges.

Conceivably, each state could establish a separate governing board for its public HBCUs, and there would be some advantages in this approach. It would ensure that the focus of the board's members was on only a few institutions and it would put people close to the problems and issues in charge. However, the political connection with the state legislature would remain, and the possibilities of racism and charges of racism would always be in the shadows if not in the open. Furthermore, the funding of a state's HBCUs in comparison with its historically white institu-tions would continue to be a volatile issue. The experience of a separate board for Southern University in Louisiana is not encouraging (Ruth, 1990). (See Chapter Nine for a further dis-cussion of the Louisiana case.)

An alternative is for several states to establish an interstate compact (as allowed under the Constitution) to operate the public HBCUs in several states. This might provide more flexibility in the adoption of roles and missions for the individual colleges, but the funding issues would remain. In fact, they would become even more complex as disagreements among the states to the compact would almost surely surface.

It seems to me that the best approach is to establish a governing board under the jurisdiction of the federal government. Congress would pass a Comprehensive Act for the Promotion, Maintenance, and Operation of Public Colleges and Universities Established for African Americans. The act would create a Commission on African American Higher Education (CAAHE).

The Commission would need to be large enough to be able to conduct its business, the volume of which would be significant. Furthermore, there would need to be enough seats to ensure that a broad spectrum of views were presented. At the same time, it should not become unwieldy. Howard University, for example, has a 27-member board, and that number might be a good one with which to start. The terms should be long enough to allow for continuity and the development of expertise, but not so long that complacency would set in. It seems to me that a nine-year term might be about right, with the terms staggered so that one-third of the members' terms expired every three years. It would then take six years for a majority changeover, balancing thereby the needs for both fresh blood and continuity.

How these people should be chosen and where the CAAHE should be located within the federal administrative apparatus might seem a boring question to many people, but, as any student of public administration would point out, it would prove quite significant in the long run. Howard University is technically located within the Department of Education (DOE), but is virtually autonomous. The DOE seems to be an acceptable place to put the CAAHE also, as much because the DOE is less likely to interfere with its deliberations as for logic. But I would think the CAAHE should be somewhat less autonomous than Howard's board.

The board of trustees for Howard University is self-perpetuating. However, Howard is a special case, being almost like a private university in many ways. These colleges would have much more of a public character, and therefore the CAAHE probably ought to be somewhat more accountable to the normal processes of political democracy. I would recommend therefore that the CAAHE president appoint the members of the board, with the consent of the Senate. Since terms would expire every three years, there would be a natural overlap of appointees of various presidential administrations. Furthermore, I would follow the Federal Reserve Board model, allowing the President to select a chair from among the members, but with the term of the chair set for four years (Kettl, 1986). This would provide a measure of accountability but minimize direct political interference.

There is the issue of whether there should be any limitations on whom the President may appoint; in particular, should only African Americans be eligible? As a practical matter, no President in the foreseeable future would appoint anyone but African Americans to such a body. However, should that fact be guaranteed by law? If so, there would have to be some legal definition of who is an African American, and frankly I find that kind of racial classification system distasteful. Perhaps, though, wording could be inserted that provided that a majority of the CAAHE must be graduates of the colleges under its jurisdiction. Even though this introduces a class bias into the law, running counter therefore to another facet of political democracy, it might be a workable compromise to the problem.

Once the CAAHE was established, any state could transfer its public HBCUs to it. This would mean the complete transfer of all legal title to property, the ownership of any endowment or trust funds and the authority to operate and manage the institutions. It would be analogous to giving a state park to the National Park Service. The state would no longer have any control whatever over the HBCUs, and the decision would be irrevocable. The schools would become federal property in perpetuity. There would be a host of administrative and technical problems that would flow from such a decision, of course (such as employee pension rights), but they are all solvable.

Two questions that arise are the role of Howard University and whether private colleges could ask to be taken over by the CAAHE. Howard University is largely the prototype for the CAAHE and a case could be made for merely converting its board of trustees into the CAAHE. However, in my view, Howard has for so long occupied such a special place in American higher education that I would personally be hesitant to tamper with its organizational structure and operation. On the contrary, though, Howard's role as a flagship institution for HBCUs might make its contribution significant for the CAAHE's success. I would leave that judgment to the officials of Howard. If they wanted in, they should be welcomed; if they wanted to remain autonomous, then they should.

Suppose a private HBCU, perhaps facing financial woes, wished to be taken over by the CAAHE? I would say once again, that the CAAHE should make that recommendation itself. There is ample precedent of ailing private institutions being taken over by state boards for higher learning. If the CAAHE thought that educational benefits could be obtained by its taking over a private school, then that should be allowed (but probably only with the approval of Congress).

The CAAHE would be empowered by the statute to exercise all the powers that governing boards of institutions of higher education normally exercise. They would have responsibility for selecting and removing chief executives, approving curricular changes, adopting or deleting programs, establishing procedures for hiring and promoting faculty members, setting admission standards, allocating budgetary resources, and so forth.

One touchy issue, legally and ethically, is whether the CAAHE could adopt hiring procedures, admissions policies, or scholarship programs that favored African Americans. It would be legally problematical whether they could successfully do so or not, depending on how the courts interpret the Fourteenth and Fifth Amendments.[1] However, from a policy perspective, I would argue that they should be able to do so if they chose. Perhaps they would choose, for example, to favor having an all-African American faculty at some institutions or in some departments and a more diverse faculty at or in others. Perhaps also they would designate some institutions or programs in which African American students would be given preference. Or, perhaps they would decide to open all the institutions to everyone on an equal basis. In any event, it would be left up to the CAAHE to debate and decide this issue. Therefore, I would think that the law ought to be written to try to give them the maximum flexibility.

---

[1] The Fourteenth Amendment contains the famous "equal protection clause" which provides that "no state shall deny any person "due process." The Fifth Amendment contains a due process clause that applies only to the federal government. However, the Supreme Court has held that this due process clause implies a measure of equal protection. (See *Frontiero v. Richardson*, 1973.) As a federal entity, therefore, the CAAHE might find itself in court if it adopted any policies which favored African Americans over others. How the courts deal with these types of cases, though, is problematical.

Since the states would be transferring the ownership and control of these institutions to a federal entity, they would no longer have any responsibility for providing funds. It could be argued that these states would be getting a significant budgetary break by taking this action. However, that raises the question of whose responsibility the HBCUs ought to be at the end of the twentieth century. That they are state-supported institutions now does not mean that the taxpayers of the states in which they are located should provide their maintenance. On the other hand, the states would be gaining the enormous advantage of having new federal installations in their states. What state would not want a new veterans hospital or a new national park built within its borders, for instance? Perhaps some type of budgetary transition could be worked out. For example, the states would have to agree to lower their budgetary contribution by 10% a year for ten years as part of the terms of the transfer. I would personally favor removing the states from the operation of these institutions as quickly as possible. This would make for a more complete break with the past.

After the transfer were executed, Congress would assume complete responsibility for regular public funding. This would make the institutions undeniably national. I would suggest that some type of bonus system should be installed, to try to make up for past budgetary neglect. For example, the national average of state support for public institutions per student credit hour could be calculated. Then, the CAAHE could be given that amount per student credit hour plus, say, 10%.

Because these institutions would be national, I would recommend that the tuition at all be the same for everyone who attended them. In other words, there would be no out-of-state fees. Thus, African Americans from all over the United States could attend these schools without financial penalty. If an African American from Seattle wanted to enroll, therefore, he or she would be treated no differently from residents of the state in which the institution was located. I would also advocate a policy that prohibited the tuition at any of the institutions under CAAHE control being set any higher than the least expensive public four-year institution in the United States. This would serve to widen access — as well as assure that Congress would not use tuition increases to alleviate budgetary shortfalls.

The CAAHE would have the complete authority to allocate the funds it received among its institutions. This would give them the tool they would need to develop institutional missions and priorities. They might decide to build one of the HBCUs into a major research university and let others emphasize undergraduate work. Conversely, they might choose to spread graduate programs around and create several specialized universities. They might even decide to consolidate or close one or more of the institutions in order to concentrate resources elsewhere. Whatever decisions they made, though, no one would be looking over their shoulders. Obviously, they would have to be accountable for the funds they spent, as are all public officials, and obviously too, they would have to abide by the law. Nevertheless, the policy decisions would be theirs alone.

Undoubtedly, various constituencies would seek to influence the Commission in one direction or another. Whatever curricular decisions they made would be controversial, as there is no unanimity among African American educators and intellectuals on that issue. They would be besieged by state and local officials wanting their HBCU to be the one awarded the most prestigious programs. They would be placed squarely in the middle of the debate over whether race or merit ought to count for more in faculty hiring and promotion. They would be faced with competition for students from historically white institutions, North and South. They would have to decide what role to accord athletics. They would have to deal with student government leaders unhappy about this or that. But all these matters are simply the nature of public life in a democracy. The point is that these decisions would be made by African Americans whose deliberations would be freed from the distorting effects of racism and not diluted by responsibilities to other institutions. That would be far healthier, I believe, for all concerned than any possible plan that keeps HBCUs as part of their respective state systems.

Let me stress that were this proposal adopted, it should not interfere in any way with the efforts of historically white universities to desegregate. Universities North and South should continue and intensify their efforts to diversify their student bodies and faculties. They should broaden their curricular offerings to insure that students are exposed to the variety of cultures that make up this country. In short, the University of Alabama and the University of Mississippi — and the University of Michigan — should still become what they should have been all along.

Conclusion

Institutions which reflect the diversity of American life are scattered all over the American higher education landscape, giving it an incredible richness and vitality. Institutions for Catholics, Presbyterians, women, Jews, Mennonites, and a host of other segments of the American population are common. There is nothing inherently wrong or antidemocratic about institutions designed to serve the needs of a particular subgroup in the United States. However, with the exception of a handful of institutions founded for Native Americans, all these institutions are private. Indeed, private institutions rooted in the African American community are similar to those cited above: no group has a large set of public institutions similar to the public HBCUs. Furthermore, no group was ever compelled by law to attend "their" institutions.

Therefore, while the modern dilemmas of public HBCUs parallel many of the dilemmas facing all other institutions representing segments of the population, they are unique. These schools occupy a special place in our system of higher education. I can see no reason why they should be viewed only as vestiges of the segregated past and therefore phased out as soon as possible. On the other hand, they cannot operate as if nothing has changed in the status of African Americans. They must find a niche, and it may not be the same niche in each case. These institutions are not all identical to each other.

I believe that the future for public HBCUs can be bright. I believe the strengths they have shown in the past fit them well for facing the challenges of the future. Their links with the African American community, and really with the American public at large, make them a vital resource for this country. But that future needs to be addressed apart from the issues facing other institutions. Because they are unique, none of them need to be governed by a board of trustees whose attention and energies are only partially devoted to these colleges. I think, therefore, that my proposal offers the best hope for building a successful future for these institutions.

References

Black, E., & Black, M. (1987). *Politics and society in the South.* Cambridge: Harvard University Press.

Greeley, A. (1969). *From backwater to mainstream: A profile of Catholic higher education.* New York: McGraw-Hill.

Grimm, F. (1991, April 29). Black colleges fear civil rights lawsuit's impact in Mississippi. *Miami Herald.*

Harrison, E. (1992, November 1). For blacks a crisis on campus. *Los Angeles Times.*

Historian sees ways to solve *Ayers* case other than closures. (1992, October 25). *Jackson Clarion-Ledger.*

Kettl, D. (1986). *Leadership at the Fed.* New Haven: Yale University Press.

Power, E. (1972). *Catholic higher education in America: A history.* New York: Appleton-Century-Crofts.

Preer, J. (1982). *Lawyers v. educators: Black colleges and desegregation in public higher education.* Westport, CT: Greenwood.

Ruth, D. (1990, February 7). Race bias ruled in Mississippi. *New Orleans Times-Picayune.*

Table of Legal Cases

Alexander v. Holmes County Board of Education, 396 U.S. 19 (1969).

Ayers v. Fordice, 112 S.Ct. 2727 (1992).

Frontiero v. Richardson. 411 U.S. 677 (1973).

CHAPTER 21

SCHOOL DESEGREGATION:
WHY IT HASN'T WORKED
AND WHAT COULD WORK

Kofi Lomotey and Richard Fossey

> Over the years, the purpose of school desegregation has become so obfuscated that many have forgotten this simple fact: Litigation for desegregation was undertaken because Blacks wanted better educational opportunities for their children.
>
> Charles Vert Willie (1988)

Background

Forty years after the Supreme Court's decision in *Brown v. Board of Education*, it is impossible to shut our eyes to this simple revelation: something has gone horribly wrong. In spite of the fact that the majesty of the U.S. Constitution was marshaled to stop racial segregation in the nation's schools and in spite of massive judicial intervention and long-term court supervision of U.S. school districts, the educational experience of many African American children is deteriorating, especially in the nation's inner city school districts and the schools of the rural South.

The evidence is all around us, and it is overwhelming. First, any assessment of racial distribution in the nation's schools — particularly our inner city urban schools — shows quite clearly that desegregation is often a fiction. In the large urban districts, student populations continue to be heavily dominated by African Americans and Hispanics. In 1986–1987, the 25 largest metropolitan districts enrolled almost 30% of the nation's African American students and Hispanic students, but only about 3% of the nation's white students (Orfield & Monfort, 1988). In many urban districts — Chicago, Cleveland, Detroit, Philadelphia, and Washington, DC, for example — a majority of the students are African American. In other districts, the student body is predominantly Hispanic. This is true not only in such Southern school districts as Dade County and San Antonio, but in many Northern school districts as well. During 1988–1989, more than 40% of the nation's African American and Hispanic students were enrolled in the 100 largest school districts (National Center for Educational Statistics [NCES], 1991, p. 4).   During 1993, these groups comprised at least 76% of the student enrollment in nine of the ten largest school districts (NCES, 1994).

Forty years after *Brown v. Board of Education,* African American and Hispanic students are often still segregated in predominantly African American and Hispanic schools. During the 1988–1989 school year, roughly a quarter of the nation's African American and Hispanic students attended schools that were less than 5% white (Tye, 1991). In the five largest U.S. districts, the school populations in a majority of the school sites are at least 80% African American and Hispanic (National Center for Educational Statistics, 1991). (See Chapter Five for further discussion of these enrollment trends.)

Northeastern schools are the most segregated schools in the country for African American students. In 1988–1989, more than 40% of the region's African American students were enrolled in schools that were less than 5% white.   Ironically, the least segregated part of the country is the South, although recent studies show a trend of increasing racial isolation for Southern African American students (Eaton, 1994).   Moreover, some of the strategies adopted to encourage desegregation may have had an opposite effect. For example, some urban districts adopted school choice plans as a strategy for achieving desegregation.   The proponents of these plans (sometimes called "magnet schools" or "options") argued that students from diverse racial or socioeconomic backgrounds could be enticed to a previously racially isolated school if the school embodied a distinctive educational philosophy or offered a specialized educational program.

In 1990, Donald Moore and Suzanne Davenport published a study on school option or school choice programs in which they concluded that these programs were not a good strategy for racial desegregation. On the contrary, the programs often had a tendency to stratify urban students by race. Selective vocational, magnet, and examination high schools tended to have a high percentage of white students compared with their overall enrollment in the school district. Non-selective low-income and low-to-moderate income schools typically admitted a high percentage of African American and Hispanic students (Moore & Davenport, 1990).

Moore and Davenport's study contributes to a growing body of evidence showing that some of the most popular strategies for desegregating schools have been unsuccessful (Singletary, 1992). Indeed, for Hispanic students, schools are becoming more segregated, not less. In 1968–1969, 23.1% of Hispanic students attended schools that were no more than 10% white. In 1984–1985, the comparable figure was 31% (Orfield & Monfort, p. 19). During the 1986–1987 school year, 50.2% of the Hispanic students in the Chicago school district attended schools that were 90–100% African American and Hispanic. In Houston, 53% of Hispanic students were in intensely segregated schools; in San Antonio, 75%; and in New York City, 68%.

Second, by a variety of standards, African American students are not doing well in the nation's schools. Dropout rates, suspension rates, and special education participation rates are high among African American students and higher than for European American students (e.g., Kennedy, 1993).

Although the National Center for Educational Statistics (1994) reports that the dropout rate for African Americans is going down, this trend masks the stark reality of high dropout rates in many urban districts. For example, in Philadelphia, where 63% of the student enrollment is African American, only half of a class of ninth graders graduate in four years (Celis, 1995). In many of the urban districts of New Jersey, the on-time completion rate for African American males is 50% or below (Burch, 1992). In New Orleans, where 89% of the study body is African American, 55% of a cohort of ninth graders failed to graduate on time in 1993 (Fossey & Garvin, 1995).

Not only are African Americans and Hispanic Americans more likely to drop out of school than white students, they are more likely to be placed in special education, where many fail to thrive. During the 1986–87 school year, African American and Hispanic American students comprised 30% of the school-age population, but they comprised 35% of the students classified as seriously emotionally disturbed (SED), 40% of the students classified as trainable mentally retarded (TMR) and 42% of all students classified as educable mentally retarded (EMR) (Gartner & Lipsky, 1989).

For African American students, their disproportionate representation in special education is especially stark. African Americans were only 16% of the total school enrollment in 1986–87, but they comprised 35% of the EMR students, 27% of the TMR students, and 27% of the SED students (Gartner & Lipsky, 1989). According to some studies, African American children are twice as likely to be placed in special education as white children (Richardson, 1994).

Suspension and expulsion rates are also higher for African American students than for white students, and far higher for African American males. A study of suspensions and expulsions in Louisiana schools during 1991–92 found that 41% of all suspensions and 58% of all expulsions were African American males, even though they only comprised 22% of the school population. African American females constituted 21% of the school population and 19% of students expelled, while white females, comprising 25% of school enrollment, accounted for only 3% of total expulsions (Kennedy, 1993).

Third, if the purpose of education is to enable our young people to earn a decent living and take their place in the nation's civic and political life, then surely the *Brown* experiment has so far been a failure for African American youth. Although the gap in achievement levels between whites and African Americans and Hispanic Americans decreased between 1977 and 1990, white children still outperform African American and Hispanic American youth at all age levels and in all subjects ("Nation's Schools," 1991). Ogbu (1986) analyzed school records of African American and Mexican American students and discovered that these students consistently performed below average. And, although African American children seem to start their educational lives with cognitive, sensory, and motor skills equal to their European

American classmates, their academic performance seems to decrease the longer they stay in school (Parham & Parham, 1989). According to Stanfield (1982), "Even in schools where the racial gap in achievement is closing, there are still extensive racial resegregation patterns" (p. 90).

Moreover, if *Brown v. Board of Education* had improved educational opportunities for African Americans, we would expect to see improvements in African Americans' economic status. A recent U.S. Census Bureau report indicates, however, that more African American families, not less, have been sinking below the poverty line in recent years. Thirty-one percent (31%) of African American families with children lived in poverty in 1993, up from 28% in 1969 (Bennett, 1995). According to the same report, African American children are three times as likely as white children to live in poverty (Bennett, 1995).

Why Have Court-Ordered Desegregation Efforts Failed?

Why has court-ordered desegregation failed to benefit African ·American children? First, after *Brown v. Board of Education* was decided by the Supreme Court, desegregation litigation gradually shifted from an effort to provide equal educational opportunities for African Americans to a political struggle for power and resources among school districts, state government, and other educational elites. (See Chapter Six for a discussion of how this occurred in Boston.) As Gary Orfield (Feldman, Kirby, & Eaton, 1994) pointed out, in the Foreword to a review of desegregation litigation:

> [T]he plaintiffs often seemed to be almost irrelevant. They were not consulted seriously about the remedy, they did not evaluate whether or not the minority children and communities actually benefited, and the remedies were terminated without plaintiff agreement that constitutional obligations had been fulfilled. What was presented as a remedy for the harms of segregation typically did not identify those harms and did not measure whether they were cured. In the court ordered cases, the remedies were basically a result of a political battle between school districts who were trying to get as much money as possible for their favorite programs and the state governments who were trying to spend as little

as possible for as few years as possible. The victims of
segregation often seemed lost in the shuffle. (p. 5)

To a certain extent, the civil rights lawyers who brought
desegregation law suits were slow to realize that improving the
condition of African American children involved far more than
placing them in classrooms with white children. As D. A. Bell
observed:

> Had we civil rights lawyers been more attuned to the
> primary goal of African American parents — the effec-
> tive schooling of their children — and less committed to
> the attainment of our ideal — racially integrated schools
> — we might have recognized sooner that merely inte-
> grating schools, in a society still committed to white
> dominance, would not insure our clients and their
> children the equal educational opportunity for which
> they have sacrificed so much and waited so long. (1983,
> p. 575)

In other words, in the struggle to desegregate the nation's
schools, the means got substituted for the ends. Desegregation
was intended to be a tool to bring about equal educational
opportunities for African Americans; despite this, school leaders,
courts and lawyers lost sight of that fact. Instead, they focused on
such things as racial balance in districts and schools, white flight,
and district-wide test scores. School leaders considered desegregation to be a success if they could say that white flight was
limited, opposition to busing was muted, or the percentage of
various racial groups in the schools was a mirror reflection of the
larger community. None of these success measures dealt with the
fundamental issue — improving the academic achievement and
life chances of African Americans.

Second, in the aftermath of *Brown,* we failed to develop new
pedagogies. Although the courts were able to require white and
African American students to be educated in physical proximity to
one another, they were unable to mandate that schools compensate
for more subtle forms of exclusion that African American children
encounter in the classroom (Graham, 1993). Today, segregated
schools have been replaced by other exclusionary measures,
including: ability tracking, a declining number of African American teachers, degrading euphemisms, a pseudo science of mental
measurement, an explosion in special education enrollments,
suspensions, and expulsions of African Americans, cosmetic

curricular changes and — in many urban schools — de facto re-segregation (Hilliard, 1988).

Third, we failed to change the attitudes and values of many of the people who staffed our previously segregated schools. When school desegregation was first implemented, many teachers and administrators were not prepared to deal with such a change and many resisted vehemently. Some teachers left school districts, retired, or left the profession altogether in order not to have to deal with desegregation.

As Dempsey and Noblit (1993) indicate, even many of the policy makers acted "ignorant" of the fact that desegregation made life harder for African Americans than for European Americans. Frequently, it was African American students, not white children, who were bused to promote desegregation. When desegregation plans required some schools to be closed, the buildings targeted for closure were often ones that were located in African American neighborhoods.

Moreover, cumbersome transfer and hiring rules, advocated by teachers' unions and designed to protect senior teachers, were largely left in place after *Brown*. As a result, it was often extremely difficult for schools to respond flexibly to changing school conditions. For example, a recent study of the Boston schools, where 48% of the student population is African American, revealed that the pupil/teacher ratio was quite low — only 13:1. However, complex work rules and collective bargaining provisions prevented the district from organizing its teachers in such a way as to take full advantage of its relatively large teaching staff (Miles, 1993). Murnane and colleagues (1991) have pointed out that complex transfer rules also hinder school districts from recruiting good teachers.

Nor did *Brown* have any effect on a disputatious collective bargaining process that often prevents educators from working together in a collegial manner. Indeed, in some districts, adversarial labor relations have largely negated such school-reform initiatives as shared decision-making or site-based management — initiatives which were designed to build trust and cooperation between teachers and administrators (Fossey, 1993; Fossey & Miles, 1992). Unfortunately, the districts where labor relations are often the most contentious are inner city districts, the very districts where large numbers of African American and Hispanic American children attend school.

Often basic reforms — abolition of corporal punishment, for example — were neglected while districts pursued superficial "restructuring" initiatives. In spite of the fact that there has been a nationwide flurry of school reform legislation, 24 states still permit school staff members to inflict physical punishment on children. Furthermore, studies have shown that African American children are the victims of this form of punishment in disproportionate numbers (Hyman, 1990, p. 57).

For example, the East Baton Rouge Parish School District, an urban district with a predominantly African American student body, has expended substantial resources and much rhetoric on school "redesign," supposedly to develop better learning environments for the children of the parish — both African American and white. Nevertheless, the district continues to practice corporal punishment and issues standardized wooden paddles from a central warehouse to the district's principals (*Advocate* staff, 1995; Beck, 1995).

In addition, although *Brown* was able to bring African American and white children into closer proximity with one another, it was unable to assure that African American children would attend school in safe and secure environments. African American children frequently attend schools and live in neighborhoods which are violent environments. And too often school administrators take a casual attitude toward children's safety, as evidenced by the common practice of covering up child sexual abuse by school employees (Stein, 1993). In many school settings African Americans find that their primary value to school authorities derives from their athletic talents, not their intellectual potential or their intrinsic human worth (Bissinger, 1990).

Third, a number of urban districts with predominantly African American student bodies are plagued by mismanagement or outright corruption — a sure sign that the care and well-being of students are being neglected. For example, in 1993, records of asbestos inspections in New York City schools were found to have been falsified (Marks, 1993). At about the same time, an investigative report was issued that described fraud and corruption by some New York City school custodians (Flamm, Loughran, & Keith, 1992; Sack, 1993). Meanwhile, in Washington, DC, school authorities allegedly overstated the district's enrollment by several thousand students (Schmidt, 1995); and, during one fifteen-month period, District of Columbia school officials hired over 100 school employees with criminal records (Report: DC schools employ hundreds, 1995). The Chicago and New York school districts have found it necessary to appoint full-time investigators to deal with fraud, waste, and mismanagement (Bradley, 1994; Schmidt, 1993).

Fourth, school desegregation efforts have failed because we have not confronted the unequal power relations in society and schools. Nor have issues of power been addressed. Power is the ability to define reality, to convince others that it is their reality, and to convince those others to act in accordance with that defined reality. U.S. society is socially stratified based upon racism, sexism, classism, and other forms of illegitimate exclusion (Stanfield, 1982). Schools, of course, are a microcosm of the larger society, and accordingly, they perpetuate these "isms." Racial and other inequities have not been addressed in society or in the schools (Fine, 1991; Ogbu, 1986).

In short, *Brown v. Board of Education* failed to achieve its promise because we lost site of the original goal — improving the lives of African American children — and because we failed to make fundamental changes in school leadership, pedagogy, school culture, and power relationships. On the contrary, the institutions and educators that our society assigned to educate African American children made few adjustments for the benefit of these children. For the schools to provide African Americana children with equal educational opportunities — which is what *Brown* guarantees — we must rededicate ourselves to transforming U.S. schools into places that nurture and respect all children.

What Needs to be Done

If we are serious about improving the academic, social, and cultural outlook of African American students, we need to begin by forgetting about school desegregation. While the notion of all students going to school together may seem ideal, it is not the solution to the critical problem of the persistent and pervasive disenfranchisement of African Americans. We need to begin to focus — directly — on the academic, social and cultural success of African American students — *wherever they may be attending school.*

Pedagogy

First, for the promise of *Brown v. Board of Education* to be fulfilled, U.S. schools must embrace a culturally equitable pedagogy. Such a pedagogy includes at least three concepts: (a) the development of culturally diverse role models in the curriculum; (b) understanding, appreciation, and respect of cultural differences; and (c) a reconsideration of traditional Eurocentric world views.

Gloria Ladson-Billings (1994) has pointed out that a culturally equitable education requires culturally relevant teaching. In essence, she argues that curricular change is not sufficient; we need to change the way we look at the world and the way we act; and ultimately we need to change the power relationships within the classroom and within U.S. society. Ladson-Billings outlines six tenets of culturally relevant teaching:

1. Students whose educational, economic, social, political and cultural futures are most tenuous are helped to become intellectual leaders in the classroom.

2. Students are apprenticed in a learning community rather than taught in an isolated and unrelated way.

3. Students' real-life experiences are legitimized as they become part of the "official" curriculum.

4. Teachers and students participate in a broad conception of literacy that incorporates both literature and oratory.

5. Teachers and students engage in a collective struggle against the status quo.

6. Teachers are cognizant of themselves as political beings (Ladson-Billings, 1994, pp. 117–118).

Other scholars, concerned about making schools work for all students, have outlined strategies to bring a culturally equitable curriculum into being. Peggy McIntosh (Noble, 1990) outlines four phases that educators may go through before a culturally equitable curriculum is in place.

1. Teaching an all-white and womanless curriculum without noticing it.

2. Putting in a few famous others who have done things worthy of study.

3. Building in issues of racism, sexism, and classism.

4. Bringing the margin to the center. Treating all voices with respect without making any superior or inferior.

All students need role models in the schools that look like them. Students need to be able to "see themselves in the curriculum" (Lomotey, 1989). This entails seeing some teachers and administrators who look like them, seeing some people in textbooks who look like them and seeing pictures of people on their classroom walls who look like them. In addition, students need to be exposed to a curriculum that reflects their culture and history.

Understanding, appreciation and respect for cultural differences speaks to the way in which we prepare teachers to teach. More often than not, teachers are only prepared to teach a particular type of child with a particular set of habits, values and cultural characteristics. The dilemma is that most children in U.S. schools do not fit this particular mold. The result is that teachers — unprepared to deal with cultural differences — do whatever is necessary to remove the perceived "obstructions" so that they can go on teaching the particular type of child that they are prepared to teach. Other children are: (a) placed in the back of the room, never to be heard from again; (b) sent to the principal's office for subsequent suspension or expulsion; or (c) recommended for special education. Simply put, we are not preparing teachers for the cultural differences that children bring to the classroom.

These cultural differences are reflected in values, in language, dress, and learning styles. For example, consider the following. If a French-speaking child is asked to repeat the phrase "the man," because of the absence of the "th" sound in the French language, the child will typically say "ze man." The teacher's response will likely be positive — an acknowledgment that the child is "cultured" and bilingual.

On the other hand, if an African American child is given the same phrase, the child will typically say "da man." There is no "th" sound in most west African languages, and the child substitutes the "d" sound. Many teachers will attempt to "correct" the African American child's pronunciation. Imagine, if you will, the impact on these two children — the French-speaking child and the African American child — when they receive their very different responses from their teacher. In the first instance, the child is encouraged, and in the latter, there is clear discouragement.

Another example stems from the premise in U.S. society that "competition for competition's" sake is a value held dear by everyone. In fact, this is an alien value for many children who are not of European extraction.

Cultural differences are also reflected in learning styles. For example, African American children (and all African children) are active learners. It is not uncommon in effective African American classrooms to see what appears to be disorder, apparent chaos and numerous loud conversations simultaneously going on (Hale-

Bensen, 1982; Lomotey & Brookins, 1988; Wilson, 1978). Yet teachers, unaware of this cultural distinction, refuse to teach children who behave in this culturally different way. And more importantly, even if they wished to teach them, more often than not, they do not have the necessary pedagogical skills.

Our society, in general, discourages understanding, appreciation and respect for cultural differences; and schools mirror that reality. For *Brown v. Board of Education* to even begin to fulfill its promise, we must begin to prepare teachers to adequately understand, appreciate and respect cultural differences.

The Role of an African-Centered Pedagogy

Thus far, we have spoken of the need for cultural equity in U.S. classrooms, and for a culturally equitable pedagogy for all school children, whether their backgrounds are European, African, Asian or Hispanic.

However, it seems clear that African American students also need an African-centered pedagogy as a fundamental part of their educational experience. Such a pedagogy is necessary for African American children to make sense of the life conditions that many of them experience and, more importantly, to enable them to resist the forces that imposed these conditions upon them (Lee, Lomotey, & Shujaa, 1993). Such a pedagogy is also necessary to "to produce an education that contributes to achieving pride, equity, power, wealth, and cultural continuity" for African Americans (Lee, Lomotey, & Shujaa, 1993).

Perhaps most importantly, an African-centered pedagogy is necessary to nurture ethical character development that leads to ethical social practice in the African American community. Certainly a critical component of an African American ethos is the restoration of the African American male as husband, father, provider, protector, and sustainer of the family.

Teachers, School Leaders, and the School Environment

For pedagogy to be transformed, school leaders and teachers must be transformed as well. This, of course, is a monumental task, and a task that federal courts overlooked while they were overseeing school district desegregation cases. Efforts were made to desegregate the teaching forces as well as the student bodies of segregated school districts; however, by and large, the courts made no effort to improve the quality of the teaching forces in the districts that went under court-ordered desegregation plans.

Various commentators have made useful suggestions for improving the quality of the teaching force and for increasing the number of African American teachers (Murnane et al., 1991). Better pay and working conditions for beginning teachers is critical, particularly in urban districts, where large numbers of poor children and children with special needs make the jobs of beginning teachers especially challenging. More time for teachers to plan, reflect, and collaborate would also help (Natriello, McDill, & Pallas, 1990, pp. 167–170), along with better pre-service and professional development training in the real-life challenges of urban schools.

On the issue of teacher quality, two problems deserve special mention. First, many inner city teachers experience "burnout" long before they reach retirement age (Dworkin, 1987). Faced with the intractable problems of inner city schools, their energy, creativity, and commitment often fade long before retirement. Second, as professional opportunities expand for the nation's best educated African Americans, schools find it increasingly difficult to attract these people into teaching. In terms of remuneration and prestige, education simply cannot compete with law, medicine, or business.

Both of these problems can be addressed by developing better incentives for recruiting dedicated teachers into inner city schools — not for a lifetime — but for shorter periods of time, perhaps three to seven years. With proper incentives, idealistic and energetic individuals could be encouraged to become inner city teachers for a few years and to leave before becoming burned out. Outstanding African Americans could devote a portion of their working life to teaching — either in mid-life, late in their careers, or prior to beginning postgraduate professional training.

Currently, teacher salary scales, teacher retirement systems, and state certification standards work together to penalize short-term teaching commitments. People who wish to teach for shorter periods of time must start at the bottom of the salary scale, with no recognition for experience in another vocation. In addition, depending on the state they live in, potential teaching recruits must complete a time-consuming series of college-level education courses before becoming certified. Finally, people who desire to spend a limited number of years teaching before pursuing another profession are faced with the prospect of losing their retirement contributions if they leave teaching before vesting in the teachers' retirement system.

What kinds of incentives would encourage high-quality short-term teachers? First, streamlined alternative certification requirements — already implemented in some states — would reduce the opportunity costs for people who wish to become teachers either before or after pursuing other careers. Second, salary schedules could be constructed that reward new teachers for experience gained outside the education field. Finally, teachers' retirement systems should be designed like those in place for college faculty members so that teachers could claim 100% of their retirement contributions when they resign, whether they teach for one year or for 30.

Obviously, we would not want all of the nation's teachers to be short-time educators. Nor would we want a school's entire teaching staff to be trained through a short-cut alternative certification process. Career teachers and instructional leaders — people who devote their entire working lives to education — should always form the core personnel of the public schools. Moreover, traditionally certified educators — people knowledgeable about curriculum, child development, and learning theory — should always be key to any sound learning environment. But public education should have a place — particularly in the inner city schools — for committed individuals who want to dedicate a few years—early in a career, mid-career or late in life — to public school teaching. Providing such places might attract some of the nation's most able African American college graduates into the teaching profession and it might also reduce the number of burned-out teachers who currently work in the nation's inner city schools.

Ultimately, however, inner city schools will not be successful because we hit upon exactly the right restructuring plan, the perfect reform strategy, or the correct school organization model. Schools will be successful when they are staffed by compassionate, energetic, and creative educators. Although U.S. schools have such educators by the thousands, too often they are in short supply in the schools that African American children attend. Moreover, educators at all levels need to reflect on their personal biographies, consider how they feel about the students whom they are charged with educating and work in concert with them to alter the status quo—to change the power relationships that exist in schools and in U.S. society.

How will we know when our inner city schools have adequate numbers of transformed educators? We will know when we see a transformed school environment. In particular, when the school environment is transformed, educators will not allow adversarial collective bargaining tactics to prevail over the interests of children. Schools will be clean and well-maintained, because the demands of the custodians' unions will be subordinate to our children's need for a safe and attractive place to learn. Corporal punishment will be abolished, along with sloppy teacher recruiting practices, fraud, and mismanagement. Children will be protected from violence, and childhood sexual abuse by school employees will be punished instead of being covered up. In short, when transformed educators transform inner city schools, African American children will find schools where they are welcomed, honored, nurtured, challenged, and kept safe.

Conclusion

We preface our concluding remarks by stating that we do not believe that U.S. public schools — as presently structured — can effectively educate African American children. Even if education is defined in its narrowest sense — merely obtaining a diploma — the high dropout rates in urban African American communities attest to the fact that public education for African Americans has largely been a failure. If education is defined as nurture, life enrichment, cultural reinforcement, and fulfillment of potential, then the failure is even more stark.

To be sure, courts have played a crucial role in desegregating schools. But in the litigation process we neglected the original concern — improving the achievement and life chances of African Americans. Although we were sometimes successful in getting white and African American children into the same school, we failed to prepare teachers who can effectively respond to children's cultural differences.

We can begin addressing this critical oversight by (a) introducing culturally equitable pedagogy in the classroom and by supporting African-centered pedagogy in districts with large numbers of African American students, (b) providing effective, competent, and compassionate teachers and school leaders, (c) by reorganizing our schools into safe and nurturing environments for children, and (d) honestly addressing the issues of inequality in society and in schools. In other words, we must do more than desegregate our schools; we must transform them into places where African American children can be successful. We are not doing that now, and every day African American children and society as a whole pay part of the price for our failure.

References

Advocate staff (1995, April 9). 'Thin' paddles ordered 1,000 at a time. *Sunday (Baton Rouge) Advocate*, p. 2B.

Beck, L.   (1995, April 9).   Principals: Many parents OK disciplinary paddling. *Sunday (Baton Rouge) Advocate*, p. 1B.

Bell, D. A. (1983). *The final hurdle: Class based roadblocks to racial remediation.* Paper presented to the Mitchell Lecture Committee of the SUNY Buffalo Law School, Buffalo, NY.

Bennett, C. E. (1995). *The black population in the United States: March 1994 and 1993.* Washington, DC: Bureau of the Census.

Bissinger, H. G. (1990). *Friday night lights.* New York: Harper Perennial.

Bradley, A. (1994, April 27). F.B.I. agent fills new Chicago post to probe waste, fraud. *Education Week*, p. 3.

Burch, P. (1992). *The dropout problem in New Jersey's big urban schools: Educational inequality and governmental inaction.* New Brunswick, NJ: Rutgers, Bureau of Government Research.

Celis, William, III (1995, March 22). Education consultant faces career challenge as Philadelphia school chief. *New York Times*, p. B7.

Dempsey, V., & Noblit, G. W. (1993). Cultural ignorance and school desegregation: Reconstructing a silenced narrative. *Educational Policy, 7*(3), 318–339.

Dworkin, A. G. (1987). *Teacher burnout in the public schools.* Albany, New York: State University of New York Press.

Eaton, S. (1994, January/February). Forty years after *Brown*, cities and suburbs face a rising tide of racial isolation. *Harvard Education Letter*, p. 1.

Feldman, J., Kirby, E., & Eaton, S. E. (1994). *Still separate, still unequal: The limits of Milliken IIs educational compensation remedies.* Cambridge, MA: Harvard Project on School Desegregation.

Flamm, S. R., Loughran, R. A., & Keith, L. (1992, November). *A system like no other: Fraud and misconduct by New York City school custodians.* New York: New York City Office of the Special Commissioner of Investigation.

Fossey, R. (1993). Site-based management in a collective bargaining environment: Can we mix oil and water?" *International Journal of Educational Reform 2,* 320–24.

Fossey, R., & Garvin, J. (1995, February 22). Cooking the books on dropout rates. *Education Week*, p. 48.

Fossey, R., & Miles, K. (1992). *School based management in the Boston public schools: Why isn't it working?* Unpublished paper prepared for the Boston Mayor's Office.

Gartner, A., & Kipsky, D. K. (1989). *The yoke of special education: How to break it.* Rochester, NY: National Center on Education and the Economy:

Graham, P. A. (1993). What America has expected of its schools over the past century. *American Journal of Education, 101*(2), 83–98.

Hyman, I. A. (1990). *Reading, writing, and the hickory stick: The appalling story of physical and psychological abuse in American schools.* Lexington, MA: Lexington Books.

Jackson, F. (1993-94). Seven ways to culturally responsive pedagogy. *Journal of Reading, 37*, 298–303.

Kennedy, E. (1993, July). *A study of out-of-school suspensions and expulsions in Louisiana public schools.* Research Report 93–1, Louisiana Department of Education, Baton Rouge, LA.

Ladson-Billings, G. (1994). *The dreamkeepers: Successful teachers of African American children.* San Francisco: Jossey-Bass.

Lee, C. D., Lomotey, K., & Shujaa, M. (1993). How shall we sing our song in a strange land? In H. S. Shapiro & D. E. Purpel (Eds.), *Critical social issues in American education* (pp. 179–193). New York: Longman.

Lomotey, K. (1989). Cultural diversity in the urban school: Implications for principals. *NASSP Bulletin, 73*(521), 81–85.

Lomotey, K., & Brookins, C. (1988). The independent black institutions: A cultural perspective. In D. T. Slaughter and D. J. Johnson (Eds.), *Visible now: blacks in private schools,* (pp. 163–183). Westport, CT: Greenwood.

Marks, P. (1993, August 8). Asbestos tests were faked, officials say. *New York Times*, p. 37.

Miles, K. H. (1993, June). *Rethinking school spending: A case study of Boston public schools.* Cambridge, MA: National Center for Educational Leadership.

Moore, D., & Davenport, S. (1990). School choice: The new improved sorting machine. In L. Boyd & H. J. Walberg (Eds.), *Choice in education: Potential and problems* (pp.187–223). Berkeley, CA: McCutchan Publishing Corporation.

Murnane, R. J., Singer, J. D., Willett, J. B., Kemple, J. J., & Olsen, R. J. (1991). *Who will teach? Policies that matter.* Cambridge, MA: Harvard University Press.

National Center for Education Statistics. (1991). *Characteristics of the 100 largest public elementary and secondary school districts in the United States: 1988–1989.* Washington, DC: U.S. Department of Education.

National Center for Education Statistics. (1994). *Digest of educational statistics 1994.* Washington, DC: U.S. Department of Education.

Natriello, G., McDill, E. L., & Pallas, A. M. (1990). *Schooling disadvantaged children: Racing against catastrophe.* New York: Teachers College Press.

Ogbu, J. (1986). The consequences of the American caste system. In U. Neisser (Ed.)., *The school achievement of minority children.* New Jersey: Lawrence Elbaum.

Orfield, G., & Monfort, F. (1988). *Racial change and desegregation in large school districts: Trends through 1986–1987 school year.* Alexandria, VA: National School Board Association.

Parham, W., & Parham, T. (1989). The community and academic achievement. In G. Berry & J. Asamen (Eds.), *Black students: Psychosocial issues and academic achievement,* (pp. 120–137). Newbury Park, CA: Sage.

Report: D.C. schools employ hundreds with criminal records (1995, April 26). *Education Week,* p. 4.

Richardson, L. (1994, April 6). Minority students languish in special education system. *New York Times,* p. A1.

Sack, K. (1993, November 17). Controls approved for custodians in New York City's public schools. *New York Times,* p. A16.

Schmidt, P. (1995, May 3). Council moving to gain more say over D.C. schools. *Education Week,* p. 1.

Schmidt, P. (1993, September 29). Throwing light on dark corners of N.Y.C.'s bureaucracy. *Education Week,* p. 15.

Singletary, C. (1992). *Academic effectiveness of elementary magnet schools.* Unpublished doctoral dissertation. State University of New York at Buffalo, Buffalo, NY.

Stanfield, J. H. (1982). Urban public school desegregation: The reproduction of normative white domination. *Journal of Negro Education, 51*(2), 90–100.

Stein, N. D. (1993, January).   Sexual harassment in schools: Administrators must break the casual approach to objectionable behavior. *Administrator*, pp. 14–19.

U.S. sounds retreat in school desegregation. (1991, January 5). *Boston Globe*, p. 1.

Willie, C. V. (1988).   *Effective education: A minority policy perspective*. Westport, CT: Greenwood.

Wilson, A. N. (1978).   *The developmental psychology of the Black child*. New York: African Research.

CHAPTER 22

A FORK IN THE ROAD FROM *BROWN*:
ANALYSES OF TWO STRATEGIES AND
THEIR GOALS FOR AFRICAN AMERICAN SCHOOLING

Mwalimu J. Shujaa and Sharon Johnson

We begin this discussion with the thought that African people whose presence in the United States is due to circumstances directly related to the trans-Atlantic slave trade, so-called African Americans, if you will, represent a cultural nationality within the nation-state. In *The Crisis of the Negro Intellectual* (1967), Harold Cruse argued that nationalism is a definite strain of thought among African American people. Moreover, Cruse laid the issues squarely on the table when he stated that this strain of thought is one that "strikes few sympathetic chords with the NAACP" — the organization that has historically epitomized the "racial integration strain" (p. 4) among African American people.

In this chapter we take the position that the "nationalist strain" and the "racial integration strain" continue to represent the two major tendencies in the collective thinking of the people in the United States who are called African Americans. The racial integration strain is supported by the nation-state's ruling elite and is proffered by the support of official rhetoric. Conversely, the nationalist strain is condemned at every opportunity. Yet, it is no secret that it was the nationalistic appeal of the Nation of Islam's Minister Louis Farrakhan that was able to hold together the united

421

front that compelled more than one million men of African descent to hold a peaceful demonstration on October 16, 1995, in Washington, DC.

Both strains of thought emerged simultaneously as strategies to determine the best course of action for people of African descent in the United States (Cruse, 1967). Although Cruse addressed them as opposites, we take the position that the differences are complementary when they are viewed holistically and in terms of the benefits they offer African people. Nationalists and integrationists have fought together on the front lines of the campaigns to win civil rights for people of African descent in the United States and to have those rights protected as called for by the laws of the land. Integrationists and nationalists alike look toward a time when a person's lot in life will not be decided by the color of his/her skin. Where the two strains differ is in the extent to which the goals they advocate require strategies which challenge the power relationships that define the existing social order.

The strategies generally employed by racial integrationists operate within limits determined by the existing social order; thus, they are social order restricted. Nationalist strategies are not restricted by the existing social order and are, therefore, social order transcendent. Jacob Carruthers (1994, 1995), using E. Franklin Frazier's (1973) critique of African American scholars, focuses our attention on how these distinctions can be understood in terms of the intellectual freedom evident in their work.

Frazier observed a sharp contrast among scholars of African descent from the United States compared to those from the African continent or from the Caribbean who participated in the First International Conference of Negro Writers and Artists held in Paris in 1956 and the Second Congress of Negro Writers and Artists held in Rome in 1959. The continental and Caribbean Africans were, according to Frazier, "deeply concerned with the question of human culture and personality and the impact of Western civilization on the traditional culture of Negro peoples" (1973, p. 55). In contrast to these questions with which Frazier believed all African intellectuals should be concerned, Frazier found that the African American intellectuals "were imbued with an integrationist point of view [and] were not only unconcerned with this question but seemingly were unconscious of the implication of the important question of the relation of culture and personality and human destiny" (1973, p. 55).

The proceedings from these meetings of "Negro Writers and Artists" were published in *Presence Africaine*. To further our explication of the distinctions that Frazier noted we will provide brief examples from two of the papers. James W. Ivy, editor of *The Crisis*, presented a paper titled "The National Association for the Advancement of Colored People as an Instrument of Social Change," in which he began by stating the "basic problem of the 15 million American Negroes is one of integration . . . Stated in different terms it is the problem of getting 145,000,000 white Americans to accept their brothers as equal" (1956, p. 337).

Ivy went on to construct this problem in a way that, in its effect, intellectually and culturally isolated the African American from the rest of the African world and disavowed the legitimacy of the struggles of the First Nations people, the autochthonous peoples of the Americas.

> The Negroes of the United States are, along with the New England Yankees and old-line Southerners, the most quintessential of Americans. They are biologically as much European as African and culturally more European-American than Afro-American. They have a Greek philosophy, an Anglo-Roman conception of law, a Judeo-Hellenic religion, and the American concept of free enterprise and the two-party system . . . It is because of his strictly American heritage that the American Negro has chosen American methods of organization, publicity, and propaganda in his fight for full equality. (1956, p. 337)

In contrast to the racial integrationist thinking expressed by Ivy, Frantz Fanon addressed the meeting on the topic of "Racism and Culture." He makes note of the strategy employed by a racist group to alienate the group that "has been rendered inferior" from its own past, but points out that "the alienation is never a complete success" (p. 127). The oppressed always fight back. Fanon's way of thinking focuses attention on understanding racism as a product of culture. He argues that "the habit should be abandoned of regarding racism as a disposition of the mind, a psychological flaw" (p. 127). Fanon goes on to consider the attitude of the person within the social group "which is enslaved, exploited, deprived of substance."

> In a first phase we have seen the occupying power legitimate its domination by scientific arguments and

the "inferior" race denying itself as a race. Because no
other solution is open to it, the racialized social group
tries to imitate the oppressor and thereby deracialize
itself. The "inferior race" denies itself as a different
race. It shares with the "superior race" the convictions,
doctrines and other assumptions concerning itself. (p.
127)

For Fanon the end of racism begins when the culturally
alienated African rediscovers his/her own culture and uses it to
render the racist arguments of the oppressor meaningless. In Ivy's
paper, one finds no such penetration into the interaction of race
and culture. Attention is given only to progress as determined by
the distance Africans lag behind whites. The issues brought to the
table by Ivy and the other integrationists Frazier observed centered
on their concerns with "increasing participation of Negroes in the
economic and social and political organization of American
society" (Frazier, 1973, p. 56). The continental African and
African Caribbean scholars, on the other hand, transcended the
colonial social orders that had sought to cultivate their minds and
concerned themselves with the future of the African world as it
stood in relation to the European world — culture to culture.

The differences in the conceptual frameworks employed by
Ivy and Fanon are illustrative of the qualities that differentiate
racial integrationist and nationalist thinking about schooling. The
social order restricted thinking reflected in the racial integrationist
strategy is concerned with the right to participate in U.S. society
on an equal basis with whites, wherever the society's leadership
takes it. In this progression the African American is expected to
be the good citizen who subordinates his/her collective interests to
the dominant interests within the society. The social order
transcendent thinking of the nationalists, on the other hand, is just
as committed to ending social inequities but its goals are not
determined by the size of the gaps that separate what white people
and African American people get from the social order. In
contrast, social order transcendent thinking is concerned with such
things as the quality of African leadership, reclaiming sovereignty,
and the means by which Africans all over the world "will restore
to their memory what slavery and colonialism made them forget"
(Clarke, 1995, p. xi). We argue that school desegregation is
reflective of the racial integration strain, while the development of

the Council of Independent Black Institutions reflects the nationalist strain.

The Fork in the Road from *Brown*

School desegregation crystallized as a legal strategy in 1950. Earlier litigation against segregated public schooling focused on making the funding and facilities provided African American students equal to that available to white students. It was in 1950, however, that Thurgood Marshall, James Nabrit, and other legal scholars made the decision to abandon the strategy of challenging segregated schools on basis of the separate but equal doctrine set forth in *Plessy v. Ferguson* (1896). The strategy they adopted challenged the constitutionality of the very concept of racial segregation in school systems. This shift in approach ultimately led to the 1954 decision by the Supreme Court in *Brown v. Topeka Board of Education* (Williams, 1987).

Scholars have expressed different views about whether school desegregation is, in fact, a necessary condition for quality schooling. Willie (1987) argues that African Americans have benefitted overall from school desegregation but points out that, although African Americans tend nationally to support desegregated schooling, there is resistance to the way desegregation has been implemented. Yeakey (1993) contends that African Americans have unfairly carried the burden for school desegregation. Hilliard (1988) points out that school desegregation strategies have left the substance of interrelated inequity functions in U.S. society unaddressed, or addressed only at a minimal level. Carruthers' (1994) view is that school desegregation became a strategy to diffuse intellectual resistance in African American communities where schools, though segregated, were important meeting places.

While school desegregation's initial focus was on the quality of schooling afforded African Americans, since 1954 the pursuit of racial balance strategies emphasizing the physical reassignment of pupils in public school districts has increasingly dominated discussions about African American education (National Alliance of Black School Educators [NABSE], 1984). Nonetheless, the majority of African American students live in the large urban centers and attend schools that are predominantly African American (NABSE, 1984; Wilson, 1991, 1992). African American students are not faring well in these schools.

African American enrollments in private schools is increasing (Benson, 1991). Much of this growth can be seen among the various types of independent African American independent schools. These enrollment patterns suggest that more and more African American families are choosing to put desegregation commitments aside, at least temporarily, to obtain quality schooling for their children in safe, antiracist, culturally affirming environments (Ratteray & Shujaa, 1987). Our interpretation of these phenomena is that growing numbers of African American families were making critical distinctions between the imperatives associated with desegregating schools and those associated with obtaining quality schooling for their children. The fact that these African American families were looking at strategies beyond the desegregation of public schools in order to obtain quality schooling represents a fork in the road from *Brown*.

School Desegregation, the Courts, and Circular Movement
    For all its legal brilliance, school desegregation as a strategy to achieve quality education for African Americans has been impotent to effect changes in the power relationships of schooling and education. Power relationships that existed prior to the U.S. Supreme Court's decisions on the constitutionality of school segregation were essentially unchanged by those decisions. Thus, while the NAACP legal strategists systematically eroded the "separate but equal" doctrine, the "integration" without power that resulted left the same authorities who managed school segregation to manage school desegregation. These authorities made the decisions about which schools would be closed, which teachers would be released, what schools children would attend, and at what pace the changes would take place.
    The oral argument given by the attorneys for the plaintiffs in *Brown I*, stated succinctly what they expected and wanted from the Supreme Court.

> We are not asking for affirmative relief . . . the only thing that we ask for is that the state-imposed racial segregation be taken off, and to leave the county school board : . . to assign children on any reasonable basis they want to assign them on. What we want from this Court is the striking down of race. Do not deny any child the right to go to the school of his/her choice on the grounds of race or color within the normal limits of

> your districting system . . . do not assign them on the basis of race . . . if you have some other basis . . . any other basis, we have no objections. But just do not put in race or color as a factor. (Wolters, 1984, p. 4)

In this statement one finds nothing that addresses the nature of white supremacy or that portends in any way to challenge the authority of white supremacists to run their schools as they always had. In fact, one can say that this argument allows the teaching of white supremacy in schools just as long as children are not restricted from attending those schools on the because of their race or color.

Brown II set the standard for implementation of school desegregation. Under the jurisdiction of district courts, the standard required a "good faith" start in the transformation of schools from a dual to a unitary system of education "with all deliberate speed" (United States Commission on Civil Rights, 1983, p. 20).

The problem was that *Brown II*, while mandating "all deliberate speed," did not define a desegregated school or provide an understandable set of mechanics for remedying a school system that was found to be segregated. The notions of the "little red school house" and "neighborhood schools," made it difficult to address with any precision the procedures necessary for the elimination of segregated schooling. In combination, with white self-interest and lack of an implementation strategy, the "all deliberate speed" formula accommodated white opposition by providing time for resistance strategies to be implemented. The forms of resistance included violence, white flight, boycotts and slow down tactics (Tate, Ladson-Billings, & Grant, 1996, p. 40).

In the 10 years following 1954, the *Brown* progeny cases (e.g. *Cooper v. Aaron & Griffin v. Prince Edward County, Virginia School Board*) established that state laws and state attempts to avoid desegregation were no longer permissible. This was an era hallmarked by "cannot" and "won't allow" court decisions that provided no accepted methodologies or court directives as to how school desegregation should be accomplished (Gordon, 1989, pp. 190–191). Left to their own devices, local white authorities dismantled schools that had historically served African American children and their communities and dismissed or otherwise rendered the services of many African American teachers unnecessary.

The steady stream of cases following *Brown* is a testament to the ingenuity and effectiveness of school officials and politicians in keeping schools segregated by race.[1] Each case revealed a new way that local and state authorities could act, and fail to act, to keep schools segregated.[2]

In 1954, the racial integration strategists did not predict that it would take 20 years for courts to deal with the infinite number of devices of massive resistance, delay and evasion adopted to avoid compliance with *Brown* and to issue orders that would result in actual integration of the public schools. They did not foresee that almost two decades would pass before many federal courts would acknowledge the existence of de jure segregation practices in northern and western school systems.

Furthermore, it was also not apparent in 1954 that the end result of two major migrations already underway at that time would bring a remarkable degree of racial segregation to metropolitan areas. The first of these migrations was the movement of African Americans from the rural South to the urban North. In 1954, African Americans were still predominantly living in rural areas. By the 1970s, they were the most urban of all American groups. In fact, more than half of all African American citizens resided in central cities, and 37% lived in the central cities of the

---

[1] *E. g., Swann v. Charlotte-Mecklenburg Board of Education*, 402 U.S. 1 (1971); *Carter v. West Feliciana Parish School Board*, 396 U.S. 290 (1970); *Alexander v. Holmes County Board of Education*, 396 U.S. 19 (1969); *Monroe v. Board of Commissioners*, 391 U.S. 450 (1968); *Green v. County School Board*, 391 U.S. 430 (1968); *Griffin v. Prince Edward County*, 377 U.S. 218 (1964); *Goss v. Board of Education*, 373 U.S. 683 (1963); *Cooper v. Aaron*, 358 U.S. 1 (1958); *Brown v. Board of Education*, 349 U.S. 294 (1955) [*Brown II*].

[2] Judge Wisdom's studied remark comes to mind: "This Court has had to deal with a variety of reasons that school boards have managed to dredge up to rationalize their denial of the constitutional right of Negro children to equal educational opportunities with White children. This case presents a new and bizarre excuse." *Bossier Parish School Board v. Lemon*, 370 F. 2d 847, 849 (5th Cir.), *cert. denied*, 388 U.S. 911 (1967).

nation's 25 largest metropolitan areas (United States Bureau of Census, 1971, p. 23). Consequently, as African Americans were migrating northward, a second migration of whites from cities and small towns to suburbs continued and accelerated. By the end of the 1960s, a large majority of urban whites lived in suburban areas (United States Bureau of Census, 1971, p. 23).

These two migrations have had a dramatic impact on the racial composition of public schools. African American students now constitute a majority of the enrollments in many cities. Accordingly, the issue in desegregation cases increasingly has been viewed as involving not merely racially segregated public schools, but more so racially segregated school *systems.*

Beginning in 1971, decisions, even by the Supreme Court majority, began to emphasize that school desegregation litigation was intended to be temporary and that the litigation should not be viewed as a vehicle for changing all of society's racial problems. In *Swann v. Charlotte-Mecklenburg Board of Education.*, the Court said that "the elimination of racial discrimination in public schools is a large task and one that should not be retarded by efforts to achieve broader purposes lying beyond the jurisdiction of school authorities. One vehicle can only carry a limited amount of baggage" (*Swann*, 1971, p. 22). More recently, in *Board of Education v. Dowell*, the Court was even more specific: "From the very first, federal supervision of local school systems was intended as a temporary measure to remedy past discrimination" (*Dowell*, 1991, p. 247). In *Freeman v. Pitts*, Justice Scalia presents the most extreme, as well as the most explicit example of the changing Court's attitude. Justice Scalia suggested that,

> we are close to that time when we should abandon the entire structure of school desegregation law because the passage of time makes it absurd to assume, without any further proof, that violations of the Constitution dating from the days when Lyndon Johnson was President, or earlier, continue to have an appreciable effect upon current operation of the schools. (*Freeman*, 1992, p. 1453)

The courts have largely attributed their own altered attitudes to the view that the passage of time has broken the causal connection between pre-1954 de jure segregation and current conditions. The Court's holding in *Freeman* is premised on the need to establish a causal connection. Therefore, in both *Dowell* and

Freeman, the district courts concluded that they should release the school boards from court supervision because existing segregation was not the caused by prior segregation (*Dowell*, 1992; *Freeman*, 1988). In both *Dowell* and *Freeman*, evidence that previously would have been found sufficient to establish causation was no longer sufficient.

Freeman involved the schools in DeKalb County, Georgia, a suburban county adjacent to Atlanta. Evidence was presented in *Freeman* that in the mid-1970s there were no disparities in educational quality based on race (*Freeman*, 1992). Only as segregation deepened and hardened in DeKalb County did the inequality similarly begin to deepen and harden.[3] In the 1980s, the district court and even the Supreme Court looked at educational inequality in a very different way. The causal link between inequality and segregation appeared to have been broken. In a chilling echo of the separate-but-equal doctrine, the courts now concluded that the solution to the racially unequal schools, which emerged as a consequence of segregation, was to improve the resources of the African American schools (*Freeman*, 1992).

Perhaps *Board of Education v. Dowell*, which involves the Oklahoma City school systems, provides even more dramatic evidence that the courts are unwilling to find causation in situations where they previously would have found it. In 1972, and again in 1986, the district court relied upon maps depicting the racial composition of the Oklahoma City school system. Apparently, the two maps are virtually identical. In the early years, the district court repeatedly found the 1972 map, and the demographics it reflected, to be part of the persuasive evidence that the Oklahoma City school system was unconstitutionally segregated.[4]

---

[3] From 1969, when desegregation began in DeKalb County, until 1975, the number of elementary schools that were at least 90% African American went from zero to five. The numbers that were more than 50% African American went from 2 to 12. The percentage of African American students in schools that were a majority African American went from 35% to & 3%.

[4] See *Dowell v School Board*, 219 F. Supp. 427, 433–43 (W. D. Okla. 1963); *Dowell v. School Board*, 244 F. Supp. 971,

In more recent years, the same district court judge found that the virtually identical 1986 map was part of the persuasive evidence that school segregation no longer existed in Oklahoma City.

The message of *Dowell* and *Freeman* is very clear:

> This is taking too long and it is too hard. We've achieved everything that can be achieved. We give up. The entire structure of the court system exists to resolve disputes. Unlike disputes brought to the executive or legislative branches, a dispute brought to the judicial branch is not supposed to arise over and over again. (Hansen, 1993, pp. 868–869)

Some observers viewed the Supreme Court's decisions in *Dowell* and *Freeman* as the end of the era of mandatory school desegregation. They perceived that "unitary" districts would be able to rapidly resume local control, dismantle desegregation plans, and return to neighborhood schools, essentially making the situation much as it existed outside the South before the desegregation era (Orfield & Thronsen, 1993, p. 759). Believing that the door to dismantling desegregation plans was now open, many school boards began filing unitary status motions (Orfield & Thronsen, 1993, p. 759).

This brief survey suggests that school desegregation as a racial integration strategy for improving the conditions of life for African American people has been unable to move in any direction that white self-interests did not want it to. The strategy was one in which African American self-interests were placed at the feet of the same legal structure that also justified African American enslavement when it was determined to be in the best interests of the ruling white elite. What we must appreciate is the fact that the decision to embark on this strategy was determined by a segment of the African American elite. It was not an accident nor was this the only strategy that could have been pursued. In fact, the inadvisability of this singular strategy was outlined by DuBois as early as 1940 (DuBois, 1973).

DuBois wrote in 1960 that the organization of African American schools and other institutions by Africans should not be abandoned in favor of racial integration. What must be remem-

---

975 (W. D. Okla. 1965).

bered, he said, "is that voluntary organization for great ends is far different from compulsory segregation for evil purposes" (DuBois, 1973, p. 152). In *Dusk of Dawn* (1995) DuBois proposed in 1940 the archetypal social transcendent strategy. We ask the reader to bear with us as we quote him here:

> This plan of action would have for its ultimate object, full Negro rights and Negro equality in America; and it would most certainly approve, as one method of attaining this, continued agitation, protest, and propaganda to that end. On the other hand, my plan would not decline frankly to face the possibility of eventual emigration from America of some considerable part of the Negro population, in case they could find a chance for free and favorable development unmolested and unthreatened, and in case the race prejudice in America persisted to such an extent that it would not permit the full development of the capacities and aspirations of the Negro race. (1995, p. 199)

The racial integrationists accused DuBois of being a "racist" for making such a statement. Yet, in it we see that DuBois is merely arguing that people of African descent should make it our responsibility to tend to what is in the self-interests of all our people. In doing so, DuBois was actually confronting the class contradictions he saw separating the interests of the "talented tenth" from those of the "whole Negro group" (1995, p. 188).

In the next section we will trace the events leading to the founding of the Council of Independent Black Institutions (CIBI) as a way of examining a social order transcendent of a strategy developed in the context of nationalist thinking.

"If Not Us, Who? If Not Now, When?": The Council of Independent Black Institutions

The Council of Independent Black Institutions (CIBI) was founded in 1972 as a national organization to unify a far flung, rapidly developing movement of Pan-Africanist oriented independent schools in the United States. CIBI's founding represented the implementation of ideas from a different ideological stream than that which guided integrationist strategies that swept African American communities during the period leading up to and following the Supreme Court's *Brown* decision. We use the emergence of CIBI to illustrate how concepts of quality education for African Americans extend beyond school desegregation when the power to define and control education is contested.

The community control of the public schools movement was an attempt by African Americans in cities such as New York City, Chicago, Los Angeles, Boston, and Washington, DC to obtain power over schools in African American communities. It marked a watershed period in African American strategies to obtain quality education by forcing confrontation over the issue of power. In her analysis of the community control of public schools movement of the late 1960s, Gittell (1969) surmised that the school desegregation movement provided African Americans "with insights into their exclusion from the school decision-making process" (p. 365). She points out further that the struggle for school desegregation highlighted both the educational and political failure of big city school districts and the unwillingness of the whites who controlled those districts to concede power. These struggles over control of schools in settings such as the Ocean Hill-Brownsville Experimental School District in New York City brought the power of whites to control African American schooling into clear focus.

Claims by African Americans to the right to control the public schools their children attended were met by organized opposition from politicians and schooling professionals. Clearly, the opposition to community control was led by whites, however when some African Americans teachers became convinced that their professional interests were threatened by community control, the movement to seize control of public schools had been defeated. This led some African Americans in the community control movement to take the position that the Brown decision had not only contributed little to African American political power over schooling, it had actually created conditions that deepened class contradictions among African Americans. In the Ocean Hill-Brownsville case, some African American teachers refused to support the local governing board's efforts to transfer what it had determined to be "uncooperative" teachers and to install African American supervisors. In 1968, Leslie Campbell (later to become Kasisi Jitu Weusi), a teacher in the Ocean Hill-Brownsville district and advocate of community control wrote:

> Suddenly along comes the "revolution" and the establishment is forced to "integrate" to try to appease the rebellious black masses. The Negro professional is

> catapulted into positions of relative importance and wealth . . . The creation of a schism between the Negro professional and black masses is the last remaining weapon of the Establishment in its effort to maintain white supremacy. (1970a, p. 26)

The attack on the community control of the schools movement further sharpened many African American activists' understandings of the politics of education and the dynamics of power. Several independent black schools were formed as a result. Kasisi Jitu Weusi left the public schools altogether and organized the Uhuru Sasa Shule (Freedom Now School) in Brooklyn in 1970. A skillful and astute organizer, Weusi was also part of the leadership of the African American Teachers Association in Brooklyn.

The echoing cry of "Black Power" became the vital spirit of the emerging independent Black school movement. Five Black Power Conferences were held between 1966 and 1970. Writing in the *Afro-American Teachers Forum* in 1967 after the Second National Conference on Black Power held in Newark from July 20–23, Kasisi Jitu Weusi expressed the fervor of many who attended those meetings.

> The dream that was born of this convention was the idea of black nationhood (here in North America) and self-determination for black people. The ideas and resolutions adopted by the conference all project toward that day when the black population of North America can say proudly, "I don't want to be part of yours, I have my own." If black power has one common meaning it most certainly means that black people have a right to and must rule and control their destinies here in America. (1970b, p. 23)

The California Association for Afro-American Education and Nairobi College jointly sponsored a conference from August 17 to 19, 1970, in East Palo Alto, California. The aims of the conference were to set up criteria for the evaluation of independent black schools and to facilitate communications between such schools. It was here that these schools were identified as "Independent Black Institutions" (IBIs) and defined as an "organized, revolutionary approach by Black people to control the development of the mind and consciousness of our community through the self-reliant process of progressive educational institutions" (Afrik,

1981, p. 14). The conference produced six fundamental concepts that characterized an IBI; these were commitments to:

     1. Communalism — the antithesis of competitive individualism.
     2. Decolonization — the acquisition of ownership and control by African people of the political, economic, social, and educational institutions which are rightfully their own.
     3. African Personality — a set of attitudes, values, and behaviors necessary for the development and maintenance of African people throughout the world.
     4. Humanism — an attitudinal and behavioral perspective which stresses distinctively human rather than material and profit concerns.
     5. Harmony — the synchronous relationship between the individual and his/her environment.
     6. Nation building — the utilization of human and material resources for community development, service, ownership, and control, which, in reality, is survival. (Afrik, 1981, pp. 14–15)

These concepts reflect the awareness of the relationship between culture and world view that existed. The movement to control African American education was taking shape around the development of institutions that would rest on values meant to sustain positive development among African people. Reflected in these concepts is an understanding of the need to deconstruct ways of thinking borne out of racist hegemony and an optimism about the possibilities of personal transformation toward becoming "new African" women and men. Additional evidence of how well the role of culture in power relationships was understood is the conference report's inclusion of the Nguzo Saba (The Seven Principles of Blackness), developed by Maulana Karenga in 1965, at the head of the list of goals identified for a proposed nationwide system of IBIs. The Nguzo Saba were intended by Karenga to be the "central focus and *sine qua non* of an internal Black value system" (Karenga, 1977, p. 21).

Shortly after the California meeting, the first Congress of African People was convened in Atlanta, Georgia on September 3–7, 1970. This meeting was actually the fifth Black Power Conference. The name was changed to illustrate that the scope of the conference was broader than the African American context (Ploski & Williams, 1990). The identification by the organizers of the continuity between the condition of African people in the U.S. and the nationalist struggles against colonialism waged by African people on the continent and in the Caribbean is a key point. "The Education and Black Students Workshop" chaired by Preston Wilcox was one of 11 convened at the Congress. Within this workshop alone, there were 10 working sessions; one of these was "Independent Black Educational Institutions." Two reports on the working session were published. The first, edited by Preston Wilcox (1970), was *Workshop on Education and Black Students, Congress of African People, Summary Report.* The second report edited by Frank J. Satterwhite (1971) was later published as a booklet titled *Planning an Independent Black Educational Institution.*

The charge given this working session was to "develop plans for establishing a parallel school system incorporating all legally, physically, and psychologically independent schools at every educational level into a national Pan African School System" (Satterwhite, 1971, p. 2).

While it appears that the participants in the working session were of one mind on the need to control the educational institutions that African people attended, there were two schools of thought about the most appropriate strategy to take. One avenue was to continue to pursue community control of public schools serving large populations of children of African descent. These schools, once under the control of the African community, would be converted to IBIs. The second strategy was to either establish new independent institutions or strengthen existing ones. It was the latter strategy that received the most attention.

A general approach to the politics of education throughout the overall workshop emphasized both the lack of power and need for power by African people over their own education. Satterwhite (1971) lists four "axiomatic" assumptions that guided all of the discussions.

1. All black educators (teachers, students, parents, administrators, and community residents) must be held accountable to the black community.

2. The education of black people must be controlled by black people whether it takes place within a white setting or within a black setting.

3. Education is a political act; its goals are people-building, community-building, nation-building. It must be directed towards

the transmission of skills, knowledge, culture, and values designed to produce a New African Man [and Woman].

4. Education must be applied as a tool in the nation-building process. (p. 6)

In his discussion of this working session Haki R. Madhubuti, in his 1973 book *From Plan to Planet*, concluded that "it is unrealistic to talk about change if you are not moving to control the instruments of change in your community" (p. 41). The above assumptions reflect analyses of the ways in which power has been successfully used against African people throughout the world. The only logical course of action perceived to be available to African people was to organize for power over their lives.

From April 21–23, 1972, the New York African American Teachers Association, an organization that propagated the concept of community control of schools, convened a meeting which planted the seed for a "National Black Education System" (Afrik, 1981). From the earnest discussions of those 28 persons, representing 14 independent schools across the country, came a mandate to form an organization whose purpose would be to produce a uniform pattern of educational achievement. Moreover, this organization would be devoted to liberatory political objectives and dedicated to excellence.

John Churchville, founder of Freedom Library Day School, one of the first of new independent schools to emerge during the era of the Black Power Conferences, was an invited attendee at that meeting. From Churchville's (1973) account of the meeting we gain a picture of the divided loyalties between public school reform and building independent institutions.

> They had a two section conference. On one side they had Black teachers in the public schools in New York concerned about survival in the public schools. Then they had other people coming to that conference who were concerned about alternative systems, and setting up methods for that. (p. 56)

Churchville, Weusi, and others already involved in building independent institutions were frustrated by the inability of the group to develop a consensus around a plan of action. A caucus of the independent school representatives was convened during the meeting to discuss what should be done. A decision was arrived at swiftly, according to Churchville's (1973) description:

> We got in a room and after fifteen minutes we came out
> of that room with a Council of Independent Black
> Institutions. Our concern was to share information,
> materials and curriculum and to have a material unity...
> (p. 57)

A national work meeting was held in Frogmore, South
Carolina from June 29–July 3, 1972 to confirm the initial mandate
from the independent school caucus at the African American
Teachers Association conference. The participants in this meeting
determined the principles, policies and programs of the organization and set up a national structure to carry out its objectives. It
was at this point that the national Council of Independent Black
Institutions (CIBI) began to function and take form. The original
statement of purpose provided that CIBI

> must be the political vehicle through which a qualita-
> tively different people is produced . . . a people commit-
> ted to truth- in practice as well as in principle- and
> dedicated to excellence . . . a people who can be trusted
> to struggle uncompromisingly for the liberation of all
> African people everywhere. (CIBI, 1972, p. 2)

It went on to state:

> The independent Black Institution is charged with the
> responsibility of developing the moral character of its
> students and staff, and of providing the clear, sane, and
> well-reasoned leadership which is imperative to a
> correct struggle for freedom and internal community
> development. (CIBI, 1972, p.2)

The formation of independent African American schools was
not a new phenomenon. The historical record shows that African
people have been creating their own schools in the U.S. since the
1790s (Ratteray, 1990; Ratteray & Shujaa, 1988). The founding
of CIBI and the movement it characterizes are historically
significant to African people throughout the world for at least two
reasons that are relevant to the present discussion.

First, we witness the employment of institution building as a
strategy for cultural liberation. CIBI's strategic use of institution
building for the independent education for African people at a time
when so many other African American institutions were caught in
the maelstrom of school desegregation has to be respected.
Institution building among CIBI members was clearly organized
resistance against the European-centered cultural hegemony and

intellectual control that shrouded school desegregation. Further, while undertaken to lay a foundation for national liberation and self-determination, institution building became a means of establishing "liberated zones" or "free spaces" where the process of education would be insulated from the cultural assault of western hegemony.

Second, we see the emergence of a network of schools for people of African descent in which there is a shift in the cultural orientation of curriculum. The efforts undertaken by the schools that formed CIBI to deconstruct European views of the world while reclaiming, recovering and reconstructing an African world view and, most importantly, to codify this process in their curricula are invaluable contributions. CIBI helped to lay a path that had been pursued earlier by Marcus Garvey's Universal Negro Improvement Association and the Nation of Islam under The Honorable Elijah Muhammad (Essien-Udom, 1962; Martin, 1976; Ratteray, 1990). This attention to the cultural context of schooling was largely missing in the school desegregation movement. A circumstance that DuBois (1973) attributed to the fear among racial integrationists that the study of African cultural history as distinct from European cultural history would set back school desegregation.

Concluding Thoughts
Our discussion has focused largely on the politics of education and the relationships of power involved in the societal and cultural contexts of schooling and education. Power is defined by Nobles and Goddard (1984) as "the ability to define reality and to have other people respond to your definition as if it were their own" (p. 107). In the context of the politics of education, Spring (1990) defines power as the "ability to control the actions of others and the ability to escape the control of others" (p. 45).

We have been concerned with the relative power to define and control the education and schooling of African American people afforded by social order restricted and social order transcendent strategies. School desegregation has provided an example of a social order restricted strategy and the formation of the Council of Independent Black Institutions has served to illustrate a social order transcendent strategy. School desegregation as a strategy does not challenge in any fundamental way the cultural and political authority of the ruling elite in the U.S. over the schooling and education of people of African descent. The African-centered institution-building model that has evolved in CIBI clearly does so by seeking power over education and schooling.

The failure to take into account differing cultural orientations and unequal power relations among groups that share membership in a society effectively obscures the contradictions inherent in assuming that education and schooling worked out in accordance with the needs of politically and culturally privileged groups will also serve the interests of groups disadvantaged within the social order. This is the reason that education and schooling do not necessarily occupy the same space at the same time (Shujaa, 1994). The cultural identity of people of African descent in the U.S. has been and continues to be influenced by the U.S. social context. It is essential to note, however, that the African cultural orientation also represents an experiential context in its own right. Thus, while African Americans exist within the U.S. social context, they also exist within the African continuity of African cultural history. This continuum has existed since antiquity. Thus, it existed before the U.S. social context and any influences that context has imposed upon African people, and will continue to exist whether the nation-state and social arrangements rise or fall.

If education is understood as the process of transmitting from one generation to the next knowledge, values, aesthetics, spiritual beliefs, and all things that give a particular cultural orientation its uniqueness, then CIBI's efforts to seize and maintain political and cultural power over the education of African people are acts of cultural responsibility. The only other option is cultural surrender, perhaps gradually, but surrender nonetheless.

Change is acceptable to those who wield power within systems only if it can be managed in a way that does not disrupt the systems' workings and power relationships. School desegregation has been a form of managed change within the general social system and its subsystems. The nature of U.S. schooling is such that African Americans are treated as one "interest group" among others to be taken into account when calculating "demands" on the system (Wirt & Kirst, 1989). We take exception to such treatment. In our view, this is an assumption of cultural neutrality in schooling. More precisely, however, it is the veiled cultural hegemony of the politically and culturally dominant elites in U.S. society.

In confronting the challenge before us, we look backward to DuBois for the guidance needed to do the work in the present that will help us to build better a future:

> We must accept equality or die. What we must also do is to lay down a line of thought and action that will accomplish two things: The utter disappearance of color discrimination in American life and the preservation of African history and culture as a valuable contribution to modern civilization as it was to medieval and ancient civilization. (1973, p. 151).

References

Afrik, H.T. (1981). *Education for self-reliance, idealism to reality: An analysis of the independent black school movement.* Stanford, CA: The Council of Independent Black Institutions.

Benson, P.L. (1991). *Private schools in the United States: A statistical profile, with comparisons to public schools.* Washington, DC: U.S. Department of Education.

Campbell, L. (1970a). The difference. In N. Wright, Jr. (Ed.), *What black educators are saying* (pp. 25–26). New York: Hawthorn Books.

Campbell, L. (1970b). The black teacher and black power. In N. Wright, Jr. (Ed.), *What black educators are saying* (pp. 23–24). New York: Hawthorn Books.

Carruthers, J. H. (1994). Black intellectuals and the crisis in black education. In M. J. Shujaa (Ed.), *Too much schooling, too little education: A paradox of black life in white societies* (pp. 37–55). Trenton, NJ: Africa World Press.

Carruthers, J. H. (1995). *MDW NTR divine speech: A historiographical reflection of African deep thought from the time of the pharaohs to the present.* London: Karnak House

Churchville, J. (1973). Freedom library day school. In Black Child Development Institute (Ed.), *Curriculum approaches from a black perspective* (pp. 45–64). Atlanta, GA: Author.

Clarke, J. H. (1995). Foreword. In Carruthers, J. H. (Ed.), *MDW NTR divine speech: A historiographical reflection of African deep thought from the time of the pharaohs to the present* (pp. xi-xv). London: Karnak House.

Council of Independent Black Institutions. (1972). Summary from first work meeting, June 30–July 3. Frogmore, SC: Author.

Cruse, H. (1967). *The crisis of the Negro intellectual.* New York: William Morrow.

DuBois, W. E. B. (1973). Whither now and why. In H. Aptheker (Ed.), *The education of black people: Ten critiques, 1906–1960 by W.E.B. DuBois* (pp. 149–158). New York: Monthly Review.

DuBois, W. E. B. (1995). *Dusk of dawn.* New Brunswick, NJ: Transaction.

Essien-Udom, E. U. (1962). *Black nationalism: A search for an identity in America.* New York: Dell.

Fanon, F. (1956). Racism and culture. *Presence Africaine, 8-10,* 122–131.

Frazier, E. F. (1973). The failure of the Negro intellectual. In J. A. Ladner (Ed.), *The death of white sociology* (pp. 52–66). New York: Random House.

Gittell, M. (1969). Community control of education. In M. Gittell & A.G. Hevesi (Eds.). *The politics of urban education* (pp. 363–377). New York: Praeger.

Gordon, W. M. (1989). School desegregation: A look at the 70s and 80s. *Journal of Law & Education, 18*(2), 189–214.

Hansen, C. (1993). Are the courts giving up? Current issues in school desegregation. *Emory Law Journal, 42,* 863–877.

Hilliard, A. G., III. (1988). Conceptual confusion and the persistence of group oppression through education. *Equity & Excellence, 24* (2), 36–42.

Ivy, J. W. (1956). The NAACP as an instrument of social change. *Presence Africaine, 8–10,* 337–343.

Karenga, M. (1977). *Kwanzaa: Origin, concepts, practice.* Los Angeles: Kawaida Publications.

Madhubuti, H. R. (1973). *From plan to planet. Life studies: The need for Afrikan minds and institutions.* Chicago: Third World Press.

Martin, T. (1976). *Race first: The ideological and organizational struggles of Marcus Garvey and the Universal Negro Improvement Association.* Dover, MA: The Majority Press.

National Alliance of Black School Educators. (1984). *Saving the African American child.* Washington, DC: Author.

Nobles, W. W. & Goddard, L. L. (1984). *Understanding the black family: A guide for scholarship and research.* Oakland, CA: Black Family Institute.

Orfield, G., & Thronson, D. (1993). Dismantling desegregation: Uncertain gains, unexpected costs. *Emory Law Journal, 42*, 757–790.

Ploski, H.A., & Williams, J. (Eds.). (1990). *Reference library of black America, Vol.1.* Philadelphia: Afro-American Press.

Ratteray, J. D. (1990). *Center shift: An African-centered approach for the multicultural curriculum.* Washington, DC: Institute for Independent Education.

Ratteray, J. D., & Shujaa, M. (1987). *Dare to choose: Parental choice at independent neighborhood schools.* Washington, DC: U.S. Department of Education.

Ratteray, J. D., & Shujaa, M. (1988). Defining a tradition: Parental choice in independent neighborhood schools. In D. T. Slaughter & D. J. Johnson (Eds.), *Visible now: Blacks in private schools* (pp. 184–198). Westport, CT: Greenwood.

Satterwhite, F. J. (Ed.) (1971). *Planning an independent black educational institution.* Harlem, NY: MOJA Publishing House.

Shujaa, M. J. (1994). Education and schooling: You can have one without the other. In M. J. Shujaa (Ed.), *Too much schooling, too little education: A paradox of black life in white societies* (pp. 13-36). Trenton, NJ: Africa World Press.

Spring, J. (1990). Knowledge and power in research into the politics of urban education. In J. G. Cibulka, R. J. Reed, & K. K. Wong (Eds.), *The politics of urban education in the United States* (pp. 45–55). Washington, DC: The Falmer Press.

Tate, W. F., Ladson-Billings, G., & Grant, C. A. (1996). The *Brown* decision revisited: Mathematizing a social problem. In M. J. Shujaa (Ed.), *Beyond desegregation: The politics of quality in African American schooling* (pp. 29–50). Thousand Oaks, CA: Corwin.

United States Bureau of Census. (1971). *Social and economic characteristics of the population in metropolitan and non-metropolitan areas: 1970 and 1960.* Washington, DC: U.S. Government Printing Office.

United States Commission on Civil Rights, (1983). *State of civil rights 1957–1983: The final report on the U.S. civil rights.* Washington, DC: U.S. Government Printing Office.

Wilcox, P. (Ed.). (1970). *Workshop on education and black students, Congress of African People, September 1970.* New York: AFRAM Associates.

Williams, J. (1987). *Eyes on the prize: America's civil rights years 1954–1965.* New York: Viking Penguin

Willie, C. V. (1987). *The future of school desegregation.* New York: National Urban League

Wilson, F. H. (1991–1992). The changing distribution of the African American population in the United States, 1980–1990. *The Urban League Review, 15*(2), 53–74.

Wirt, F., & Kirst, M. (1989). *The politics of education: Schools in conflict* (2nd ed.). Berkeley, CA: McCutchan.

Wolters, R. (1984). *The Burden of Brown: Thirty Years of School Desegregation.* Knoxville: The University of Tennessee.

Yeakey, C. C. (1993). The social consequences of public policy. *The Journal of Negro Education, 62* (2), 125–143.

Table of Legal Cases

Brown v. Board of Education of Topeka, Kansas (Brown I) , 347 U.S. 483 (1954).

Brown v. Board of Education of Topeka, Kansas (Brown II), 349 U.S. 294 (1955).

Cooper v. Aaron, 358 U.S. 1 (1958).

Dowell v. Board of Education, 782 F. Supp. 574 (W.D. Okla. 1991).

Freeman v. Pitts, Civ. No. 11946, Slip op. at 27-28 (N.D. Ga. June 30, 1988).

Freeman v. Pitts, 112 S. Court. 1430 (1992).

Griffin v. Prince Edward County, Virginia School Board, 377 U.S. 218 (1964).

Plessy v. Ferguson, 163 U.S. 537 (1896).

Swann v. Charlotte-Mecklenberg Board of Education, 402 U.S. 1 (1971).